SOUL OF A MAN

EDITION II

A COLLECTION OF SHORT STORIES, POETRY, AND THE STORY BASED ON POIGNANT SCREENPLAY:

Souls Of Black Men

Copyright © 2024 by Rodney R. Rhodes

ISBN: 978-1-77883-435-6 (Paperback)

All rights reserved. No part of this publication may be reproduced, distributed, or transmitted in any form or by any means, including photocopying, recording, or other electronic or mechanical methods, without the prior written permission of the publisher, except in the case brief quotations embodied in critical reviews and other noncommercial uses permitted by copyright law.

The views expressed in this book are solely those of the author and do not necessarily reflect the views of the publisher, and the publisher hereby disclaims any responsibility for them. Some names and identifying details in this book have been changed to protect the privacy of individuals.

BOOKSIDE Press

BookSide Press
877-741-8091
www.booksidepress.com
orders@booksidepress.com

Contents

Souls Of Black Men

Chapter One: The Youth 8
Chapter Two: The Meeting 10
Chapter Three: Jalen & Percy 29
Chapter Four: Steve, Lawrence & The Reverend
Clayton 35
Chapter Five: Carmen & Allen 42
Chapter Six: The Meeting Reconvenes 47
Chapter Seven: Reverend Clayton's Home 56
Chapter Eight: Coming Together 60
  • *Diner On The East Side Of Detroit—Mid
    Afternoon* *61*
  • *Reverend Clayton's Home—Several
    Mornings Later* *65*
Chapter Nine: Redemption 68
  • *Auditorium Of Highland Park Community
    High School* *68*
  • *Sunday Morning—Reverend Clayton's Church* *76*

Falling in love in 30 Days

Falling in love in 30 Days 79
Meaning of a Father 104
Can I sculpt U? 107

Family Existence 109
This Time I'm Going to Love Me 111
The Struggle 113
A Firm ASS Whipping- No More Affirmative
    Action! 115
Hero 117
Air 118
My Big Brother Could Rap 119
Every Time the Wind blows think of Him 121
All Along 123
Cupid's Arrow 124
Who's next in line, your son or mine? 125
Out of This World 128
Priceless 129
1+1 130
A True Poem (in the making of Randy) 132
Deeper than a Video 134
From a Dream to a NIGHTMARE 135
Black Folk – Calling 911 138
Just Keep Coming! 140
Miracle Worker 142
Bridging the Gap 144
Taste Great and less Feelings 146
You Better Date Calvin (Mickey D's Guy) 147
My Greatest Dance Partner 149
Destiny 150
Your Company I don't Need! 151
I'd Rather Walk in my HOOD 152
Flower 154
Passion for Lust 155
Blame Me 156
Sabotage 158
Me, Myself, and I. What a Lie! 160

To Rodney R. Rhodes from Donald Goines: You Better Man Up! 162
Difference in US 164
In the Blink of an Eye..166
Today 167
Hired Help...168
Numbers 169

The Wise Man On The Corner Series

Family

Family 173

Drugs

Drugs 181

Education Is The Best Defense
Candice Blood

Candice Blood..191

Souls Of Black Men

CHAPTER ONE

THE YOUTH

It's summer time in Highland Park, Michigan. A city known for its historical landmarks, such as the Henry Ford Plant. Now, travel with me down Davison Freeway, just pass Highland Park Community High School, and various shops. There you will find six teenage boys, Steve, Percy, James Clayton, Lawrence, Allen, and Jalen. They are all standing outside an old abandoned building in the heart of Highland Park. The six teenagers are watching a drug transaction between a baller and a crack head.

One of the neighborhood boys, Steve was the first to make a comment. Steve said, "That's dumb! Why keep killing him! He's already dead! At that time, Steve was a dark-skinned brother, who was very poor and considered unattractive by his peers. Then Percy looked on in amazement. Percy excitedly shouted, "Man, that's power! See that money and that jacket. Goods and 'cervical." Then James Clayton said, "What?!? That's not Coochie! You mean "goods and services." He'll pay one day. Ain't no fun when the rabbit got the gun. One day he'll be at the losing end. He's just killing God's children with those drugs! That's when Lawrence looked at them and said,

The Youth

"Haven't we learned yet? We're still making the same old mistakes. I'm going to be a better man. I'm going to make a difference, just wait and see."

Next, Allen waded in on the conversation. Allen said, "Me too, I hate this! Our people are falling down quick." Then he was interrupted by a lady walking down the street. She turned out to be a female drug addict. She said, "I got the baddest mouth in the city; can I blow you for a rock, just a lil' taste? Come on man, I promise I'll' make it feel real good. In unison, all the guys said, "Hell no, we ain't into that! In discuss, Jalen said, "Damn Crack heads!! Go clean yourself up, tramp! Then he looks around at his boys, and he quickly changed his tone of voice and said, "I mean lady." The guys return to their conversation as the woman walks away.

Percy hit James on the shoulder. Then Percy enthusiastically said, "I keep saying' there's power in that dope, man! Power! Did you see what she was willing to do, just for a rock?" Then James quickly corrected him. James said, "The devil has power too, but Jesus has the greatest power, and the best laid plans. Let's go, this is whack! Let's go get some Coneys and fries."

Chapter Two

The Meeting

Twenty years have since passed; and Detroit has even more landmarks. Such as, the Compuware Building, Detroit Institute of Art Building, Renaissance Building, the Whitney Restaurant, Joe Louis Arena, the Casinos, and of course the legendary Motown Museum.

The six young boys have now become powerful men. These men grew up in Highland Park, Michigan, a city that was crumbling. They were on the rise in Detroit, a city that surrounds the inner city of Highland Park, commanding power, money and respect. They came together for a meeting of The Black Man's Society, an organization that was founded by them; when they were young, up and coming. **James Brown said it best, "It's a man's world, but it wouldn't be nothing, without a woman or a girl."**

The meeting takes place at Bakers Keyboard Lounge, historically the oldest Jazz club in the world. The time is 3pm on a Friday. This is the location where six childhood friends hold their first of the month meeting of The Black Man Society. Steve arrives first. In walks Steve, the President of the Black Man Society. **Steve** is a dark skin brother,

The Meeting

who was very poor and unattractive when he was younger.

Now, he's full of muscles, with the chiseled face of a handsome king, and very wealthy. He finds it hard dealing with success and good looks, because of his prior hurt. He owns a very lucrative construction company, the biggest in the city. Steve is the first to walk up to the table, followed by Jalen and Rev. Clayton. Steve shakes hands with Jalen, next Rev. Clayton. Then Steve say's, "What's up Jalen?" Jalen says," Nothing much bro." **Jalen** is the writer, who always tried to be the best. But, he grew into everything by trial and error. He has had his heart broken on many occasions, even though he was the reason. The relationships never worked, because he always hid the fact that he needed a Woman's Company to write. He was a good man with lots of money, but a terrible mate. Then Steve walks up to Rev. James Clayton. He said, "How are you doing Rev. Clayton?"

Rev. Clayton replies, "I'm so truly blessed and how about you?" The good **Rev. Clayton** was a God fearing man whose wife can't stop cheating. He will not divorce her. Due to the fact, that he loves her so much, and his family means the world to him. Besides, what would the members of his million dollar mega church think if he did? Steve replies to Rev. Clayton. Steve said, "Good. I can't complain, if you ask me again, I'll tell you the same. Ha, Ha! "He laughs. Rev. Clayton shakes his head at Steve, smiles and turns to Jalen. Then Rev. Clayton asks, "How about you Jalen?" Jalen replies;" I'm holding on to dear life trying to make my wrongs right." Then Rev. Clayton tells Jalen to put God first and He'll make it right. Jalen nodes his head and says," No doubt." Steve looks around and says, "Where's the rest of the fellows?" Jalen answers him with a smile on his face; and says," You know they are always on "CP" time, Ha. Ha."

About that time, Carmen comes up to the table and asks the guys for their orders. **Carmen** is the beautiful waitress that brings the gentleman drinks. She has a vivaciously genuine personality and she is also in her last semester of nursing school. Carmen hands them menus. Then she reaches in her pocket and pulls out a pad to take their orders. She then reaches in her hair and pulls out a pen. With pen and pad in her hand; she asks, "Hi, guys what would you like?" Jalen looks Carmen up and down. Then he said, "I don't think it's on the menu." Carmen rolls her eyes. Then Rev. Clayton said, "Come on now Jalen, let the woman work."

Jalen said, "Dang… Ok, let me have a Dirty Martini and your phone number?" Then he winks his eye at her. Carmen sarcastically said, "Ok, a dirty Martini and the wrong number." Then, she turns and smiles at Rev. Clayton. Carmen asks, "And you kind sir?" Rev. Clayton replied, "Well, I'll have a glass of tea, extra lemon and sugar please." And he smiles. Carman asks, "Sweet n' low or pure sugar?" Rev. Clayton says, "Pure Sugar." Then Carmen looks over at Steve and politely said, "And for you?" She caught him off guard and Steve said, "Ohmmm…let me have ohmmm a Bud lite!"

Jalen started mocking Steve and said, "Ohmmm, let

The Meeting

him have a shot of Ohmmm mm1800 tequila! Then Jalen laughs. To get Jalen's attention Rev. Clayton firmly says, "This is business right? Maybe after the meeting, but not now! We have three more guys coming. We can wait… I mean you guys can wait to get plastered after the rest of the group gets here." Carmen returns with the drinks. She is holding her order pad in her hand, and tapping her foot. Then she says, "Ok, would you like an appetizer with your drinks?" Steve replies, "Let us have the W.C. Handy Platter please." In walks Lawrence and shakes hands with all of the guys.

Lawrence is a high powered attorney who loves young women. He always has two or more to keep him satisfied. He doesn't want to be held down. His favorite saying is, "I don't want nothing old, but money!" Only now, he's growing old, tired and can't keep up with the young ladies. Lawrence looks at the guys and says, "How are you fine Gentlemen doing; on this fine day?" Steve raises his eyebrow and said, "Late. You are always late Lawrence! I don't know how you can be a lawyer, your clients will be locked up or dead by the time you get to the court room." With a smirk on his face, Lawrence said, "For your info, I sue hospitals and companies. I go after big bucks. And unless your name is Percy or you have Percy kind of money, I am going to be tardy and I just might be absent."

Percy had just walked in and overheard the reference to him and his money. Percy angrily said, "Man stop putting me out there like that! I have paid my dues. Nobody has the right to belittle me. Do you hear me? Percy grabs

Lawrence's collier and said, "I am not laughing. Do you hear me?" **Percy is** the ex-drug dealer, who has been in and out of jail many times for drug smuggling. He's rich beyond thought. Average looking and ruthless to those he doesn't know. Women absolutely adore him; because they find his "Bad Boy" image extremely desirable. Though he's not chasing them anymore, because he's now attracted to Men!

Lawrence shrugs his shoulders. Then Lawrence said, "I'm sorry man. I didn't mean anything by it. Percy ignores Lawrence's apology and he turns to the others. Percy proceeds to say, "What's up you all"?" Steve hits the table with his gabble. Steve says to the others, "Calm down. This meeting is about to begin." Then Steve looks around the room confused and said, "Where is Allen? He is never late." Then some of the others look around, and shrug up their shoulders as to say, "I don't know?"

About that time, Carmen walks back over to the table to deliver the first round of drinks. She takes out her pad to take the orders of the new arrivals. Carmen turns and ask Lawrence and Percy, "What will it be gentleman?" Lawrence notices how stunningly attractive and young Carmen is. Lawrence replies, "Red bull and Hennessey." Jalen looks at Lawrence and says, "You are always trying something new." Lawrence winks his eye and said, "Yeah right. I don't like nothing old, but money." Then he laughs.

Meanwhile, Rev. Clayton shakes his head at Lawrence. Then the Rev. said, "One day you won't like yourself." Then Lawrence sadly looked into the bottom of an empty

The Meeting

wine glass and said, "Truth be told, I don't like me now." The others confusedly turned and look at him. Jalen said, "I don't either." Jalen is always playing the joker. Then Jalen laughs. Carmen said, "Ok. Are you guys finished with the dog fight?" Then she pulls out her pad to take orders and gives them the others menus. Carmen looks over at the handsome and very desirable Percy and she says, "May I help you, sexy?" Percy is obviously tired of women coming on to him. Percy replies, "Yes, my name is Percy and you can help me. I want a bottle of <u>Cristal</u> Champagne chilled and some olives on the side please?" Carmen sequences her eye and says, "Ok, coming up!"

Allen rushes in looking ragged and tired. **Allen** is an hourly electrician at the Chrysler. He makes about a $160K grand a year. Allen would take the woman, who works at IHOP; if she would just talk to him. Allen is a good looking man, but he is also shy. Allen somberly says, "Hey, everyone." Percy puts his hand on his shoulder and says, "My man Allen, What's up? Then he stands and shakes Allen's hand. Rev. Clayton approaches Allen and says, "Hi! God's child. How's the family?" Lawrence is looking at Allen disgustedly. Then he said, "Man, stop working so hard and eat." Jalen interrupts and says, "Allen my man how's that fine sister of yours? Jalen smiles and said, "Tell her I said, Hello. And by the way, I need your Chrysler a-plan. I want a Viper." Steve said, "Look here, we are a gentleman's organization, we must dress the part. Allen, next time slacks with the 'blazer!' 'Oh, and hello my old friend.

Carmen returns with the food and the drinks. Carmen then turns to Allen and says, "What will it be?" Allen said, "A water please?" Percy mildly shouts, "Come on Allen, just water? Allen wipes his hand on his forehead. Then he said, "I have to work. I'm working twelve hour shifts this week." Percy downwardly shakes his head and makes the "Ohm…" sound. The others just look at each other, then the floor.

There is a moment of silence, because the meeting is about to start. Steve has the floor. Steve recites The Black Man's Society Creed: We are here, the Power of Colored Skin. May we come together as black men for us to be a greater people with the love of God, community, family, and friends. Let those who oppose carry the weight of our plight. Only togetherness will hold us tight. Love will be our might. All in favor raise thy right hand and repeat after me: Black Men!

Everybody in unison said "Black Men! Then Steve said, "We will have Rev. Clayton to lead us in the *Lord's Prayer."* Rev. Clayton said, "May we all bow our heads. Then Rev. Clayton began to eloquently speak and he said, "OUR Father, which art in heaven. Hallowed be thy name. Thy kingdom come. Thy will be done in earth, as it is in heaven. Give us this day our daily bread. And forgive us our debts, as we forgive our debtors. And lead us not into temptation, but deliver us from evil: For thine is the kingdom and the power, and the glory forever. A-men."

Suddenly, Rev. Clayton holds his head in his hands and starts to cry. The others huddle around him; hugging

The Meeting

and patting his back to calm him down.

Rev. Clayton puts his head down and reaches into his jacket for a handkerchief. Dripped in tears; Rev. Clayton said, "I'm sorry brothers." He pauses and continues. "Jesus help me. My wife is tearing me down. I can't hold my tears. She's stealing my joy!" Allen with a worried look on his face asks if she is alright. He said, "She's not sick is she?" Rev. Clayton blows his nose and gets control of himself. He waves his hands and said, "No. I...I'm sorry, forgive me brothers." Percy approaches him and said, "No, Rev. We are your brothers. Tell us what's wrong. Don't you shut us out? Talk to us. Let it go, baby."

Then Rev. Clayton said, "Thanks brothers, but it's not your problem. I'll take it to Jesus." Allen empathically looks him in the eye and says, "Jesus is in us. And we love you, so lay your burdens down. Remember, God will send an angel in the form of men. You cried for a reason. It is said tears have a way of washing away the hurt. So cry! Remember, you are a man, not Jesus. But, even Jesus wept on the cross..."

Rev. Clayton sits down. The others sit down as well. They look at the Rev. waiting patiently for some kind of response. Rev. Clayton sits still for a few minutes, to get his composure together. Rev. Clayton reveals the true source of his agony. He blurts out, "My wife has been fooling around on me. The others gasp and look at each other. He continues and says, "She says I'm too busy, or always at church. If it's not service, a wedding, a funeral, or a baptism; it's the hospital! It's everything, except her and the children." Upon finding this out Lawrence becomes highly upset and hits his fist on the table. Lawrence in his lawyer demeanor states, "Oh, Yeah!

But, she's got everything a woman want; a big house, big cars, diamonds, furs, whatever she wants. So, why is she crying? I know at least one hundred ladies, who would love to change spots with her." For years, Jalen has known the Rev. 's wife, and always thought she was a fine respectable lady. So, he began to reason in his mind. Jalen slumps back in his chair and calmly explained, "Man, she needs her man. The man works more than Allen. Rev. take it from me, I deal with women all day. They will stray when the cats away. So, maybe you should slow your roll Rev. It will be difficult, but not impossible."

Rev. Clayton shakes his head. And then he said, "It's not that easy." He goes on to tell them, "My flock depends on me. Mothers are crying, because their kids are on crack. Fathers are not at home. People needing faith and my wife is losing faith in me." He hunches his shoulder and asks, "How, can I tell someone that I can't do their mother's eulogy, because my wife and I have a lunch date?" Steve looks at his good buddy and says, "Pray about it man. It's hard being a black man. The decisions we face being in love, trying to be strong." Steve pauses and thinks about his own sad situation. Then he said, "Rev., I don't know when someone loves me for me, or my money?" Next, Steve said, "I've let go of some real good black sisters, because they are always talking marriage after three months of dating. They are talking about rings, and kids, and they don't even

The Meeting

know me or my background. We were so poor; my family couldn't afford a carrot. Let alone, a 6 karat diamond ring! So, now you have to prove your worth to me, and that's not so easy to do." Lawrence shakes his head.

Then Lawrence replied, "That's why I date the young ones. Shoot, I give them a little money, some clothes, and they let you do anything, say anything and leave anytime. Our people have changed. Men have become soft; they want love just like the love women want, but unfortunately most women are just like those who raised them...BITTER! Now women are seeking designer names, money and a good time. Face it, Ebony, Jet and Essence of her Vagina got you out of control! Jalen nods in agreement.

Jalen exclaimed, "I can dig that! They come off as your greatest friend, but soon as you say, "I love you" the chase is over. Women got their own agendas. You better have your strength. They want the Percy's: the ballers, the rough-neck brothers who never change; always running from something; never to be caught by anything but a jail cell or a bullet."

Percy quickly becomes offended by Jalen's remarks. In a defensive voice, Percy said, "For one, leave my name out of your mouth! Brothers...our sisters want somebody to take control. No weak ass crying or asking; but 'taking' kind of brothers! That's why they like the rough-necks. The music industry sells propaganda to enslave our people. I know guys who go to jail for 10 years and have 15 children. They drove the best, drank top shelf and didn't have a job to speak of! You see, it's not just our women; it's ALL of

Soul Of A Man

us; the parents, reverends, teachers, politicians, ME and you. Since we are talking about me, let me do it for you. Big Percy went to jail and got raped! I have been living on the down low for years." Percy stops to look each one of them in their eyes. Then Percy goes on to say, "How could I be a real man to any woman with my own demons chasing me every day? That's why it is so easy for me to say "no!" They all gasp and look on in astonishment at Percy. Their eyes wide and mouths open.

Reverend Clayton was blown away by his statement. Then he said, "Not you, Percy!!" Percy nods his head and replied, "Yeah, me...the one who sold much dope to our people. Karma does come and greet you one day. You reap what you sow. Rev., the loan I gave you that started your church was dope money. See, these dealings you had with me. This is what's bringing about your bad Karma; your wife is just part of your pay back."

Allen disagrees and shakes his head. Allen began to explain, "No, Percy that started your healing. You knew you were wrong, but you tried to make amends in your own way. See, we all have souls. God will let you get lost, so that you can find your way back home...to Him. Rev. Clayton raises his hands to the Heavens and he shouted. The Rev. said, "Sinners are we, but you must remember, the ultimate price has already been paid. He gave HIS only begotten Son!" That's when Lawrence began to tell his own ugly truth. He confessed that his life of luxury, wining and dining was not all it's cracked up to be. Lawrence said, "I'm tired too, I'm slowing down, my body is so weak. I

The Meeting

can't even make love anymore without a little blue pill! Drinking till I'm in a drunken stupor, blowing meetings off, thinking I'm God's Chosen One!" Then he lowers his head and his demeanor changed. Lawrence closed by saying, "What has become of me?"

Allen puts his hand on his buddy's shoulder. Then Allen said, "We all need God's healing hand. It's not what is in our pockets or pants; it's what's in our hearts, minds and souls. We come from little of nothing. As brothers, we must talk to one another. Show character. I don't care about any damn money! I care about love. We forgot how to be a team; singing "We Shall Over Come." Now, we replaced the "we" with "I."

It is now, mid-afternoon at the Barkers Keyboard Lounge. And the lovely, Carmen has been watching and listening from the bar. She's convinced that the guys could probably use a break in the conversation. She slowly walks over to the table, smiling like she knows nothing of the deep conversation that just took place. Carmen asks, "Would you guys like another drink?" Everyone instinctively replied, "No, just juice!"

Carmen is taken back by their answer, and she said, "Wow, what happened here?" Carmen looks at each of the guys and her smile slowly fades. Jalen gets up and walks over to Carmen. Then curiously he said, "Sweetie, what kind of man do you want? Carmen pauses as if pondering the question. Carmen responds by saying, "I need and want a God fearing man. The strongest man is one, who believes all things are possible in HIS realm, HIS light and

HIS vision! One who knows that he can make a mistake, but who's willing to change for the better in order to make this world a better place by doing right." Then she smiles.

Steve said, "Carmen, can you sit for a moment? We need a lady's input on our discussion. We have been a little misguided going through life for a while without some much needed closure. Can you give us a little feminine advice?" Carmen responds by saying, "I'd love to, but you'll have to ask my boss, Mr. Porcher." Carmen points to the man standing behind the bar. Then Steve said, "No doubt. I'll go talk to him." Steve gets up and heads over to the bar, to speak to Mr. Porcher. Jalen turns to speak to Carmen and gets a little personal.

Jalen said, "How old are you?" Carmen smiles and said, "A lady never tells." Next, Jalen asked, "Okay, Lady, how did you get so much old folk wisdom?" Carmen replied, "Well, from a gang of good ole folks; who had my best interest at heart; my Mom, Dad and a host of family. It takes a village to raise a child; and the Bible to make you a well-rounded, stable adult." Steve makes his way back over to the table.

Then Steve sits down and asks Carmen, "What do you do, besides waiting tables?" She said, "I'm studying to become a Nurse. I enjoy helping people and God knows people need a lot of help." Jalen anxiously asks, "That's so awesome. Are you married or engaged?" Carmen hesitates at first. Then she decides it's okay to be open and honest with them. Carmen honestly said, "No. My heart wants a man, but I don't have time right now to give a relationship

The Meeting

what it needs to be successful. So, I'm going to wait. My eyes are on the sparrow. Besides, bills and my studies keep me grounded. And there are a lot of thieves, liars and smooth operators out there, much like you gentlemen...or at least some of you!" She glances over at Jalen, and smiles. Allen makes the Ohm look with his eyes; and perceives her as very good observer. Allen asks, "How can you tell that about us on sight?" Carmen said, "Honestly, I can't but that's how men with power feel about themselves. They work so hard to be the best. Sometimes it brings out the worst in them. They have no patience for anyone else."

Allen comments, "So, when you achieve your goal, will you be like us or like them?" Carmen gets comfortable and crosses her legs. Then she looks him in the eye. She politely said, "Look, we all need someone. Adam is a rib short and God is never wrong. We try to take things away from the Good Book, to uphold our short comings. We do a lot of rewriting, but we fail when we do." Allen says, "What about children?" Carmen spoke with an uplifting voice and said, "What about children? I don't have any children. I figure as long as, we can still have them. God has not given up on us. The next generation could make a difference."

Reverend Clayton decides to weigh in on the conversation. Rev. Clayton said, "You should visit my church. I need beautiful people like you in my ministry. Carmen thanks him and replied, "That would be so very nice, I need to make more time for the Lord. That is where my blessings lay. And I sometimes get so caught up in making it..." Steve interrupts and asks, "What's "making it?" Lawrence said, "You know, having money is not always the key to success. Carmen, keep your outlook positive and you'll make it very far. You truly are a breath of fresh air. I was losing hope for a good woman until I heard what you had to say today. Thanks for restoring my faith in women, at least."

Carmen looked in shook and said, "Why is that? There are so many of us out here. If you take the time to look, really look, not just at our backsides, but look at us. See us for who we really are. If you want to know, look at our family. The apple doesn't fall too far from the tree. Look at the roots, the branch and the other apples that are born of that tree. If the majority is bad, then that person will undoubtedly have some of those traits. Then sometimes... just sometimes, you will find a diamond in the rough. One who is as sweet as Apple Pie." Steve respects her wisdom. So, he decides to ask Carmen for a little insight to help him with a relationship matter; and Steve said, "When you have a lady who's not what you thought she was. What do you do?" Carmen responses by saying, "Often times, it's what we thought; because, it's what we want to see, or want them to be. First, you must talk to her; but not at her, and try to get on the same page. She might feel the same way about you. Communication is the key to everything. See, we are so into ourselves; that sometimes we forget about each other. It takes two to be in a Relationship; and it always helps to be friends first. Love is kind and forgiving and it has no shame. It takes

The Meeting

unconditional love to understand "love."

Allen is intrigued by her mind; and he said, "I really like your philosophy. It's very deep. Rev. Clayton says, "Yeah, so Christian-like." Carmen shrugs her shoulders. She said, "I try to be." Allen said, "Your efforts are very admirable." Once shy, Allen looks Carmen directly into the eyes, as if he was seeing her for the very first time. Allen looked at her, as if she was the only person in the crowded restaurant. He said, "You are beautiful, too." They both dreamily stare at each other. The others notice and look at each other. They smile knowingly and nod as if to say, "It's about time." Carmen blushes and said, "Why, thank you. You aren't so bad yourself. Allen asks, "Would you like to get coffee one day?" Carmen shakes her head, snapping out of this love trance. She says, "Would your better half approve of that?" Allen gets flustered and says, "No. I mean yes. I mean, I'm a whole. I don't have a better half; I'm kind of a lot like single..." Jalen mildly shouts, "I'm single, too!" Carmen looks at him with her eyebrow raised and said, "And!?"

Jalen said, "And what? I'm not good enough?" Carmen said, "You are so full of yourself. You might even be a gift from God. But, you seem like trouble to me. So you're not MY gift from God." The others laugh and smile because they know she's right. Steve said, "She called a spade, a spade. And, she's the grand prize winner for having guessed the character correctly." Jalen sorely said, "What do you mean? I'm love. I'm kind and nice." Steve said, "To every woman with a big butt and a smile. That's your problem.

You stare at women all the time, even when you are with another woman. It's just in your nature." Lawrence said, "He's right, Jay, that's you to the tee: a big old flirt; always wanting something better!"

Jalen said, "What's wrong with that?" Carmen, "Everything! Why would you keep looking for someone better, when you're not making yourself better? Maybe your problem is yourself. You are searching, looking outward, but needing to look inward to find yourself. Slow down, my brother. Be patient, quality is better than quantity." Rev Clayton exclaimed, "Lord, have mercy! Preach, my sister, educate him now!" Jalen, "I'm alright with myself. I'm alright; I know my flaws." He pauses and swiftly becomes irritated. Then with a nasty tone, Jalen said, "My wife is not cheating on me!" The others look at Jalen, and are angry and disappointed at his rude outburst. Percy shouts, "Fool! Why did you have to go there? That was not right, you little punk!" Jalen, said, "I know that YOU of all people did not call ME a punk! Isn't that the pot calling the kettle black? Sissy!"

Now, Percy and Jalen stand up with fists balled, glaring at each other, with obvious rage boiling within. Holding back his rage, Percy said, "Boy, don't make me hurt you! You know I will." Clinching his fist tighter, Jalen said, "Go for what you know. My mama didn't raise no punks! Percy said, "Oh, now you want to put my Mama in it?

Steve, being the peace maker, holds his hands out to keep the two apart. Steve said, "Hey, cut the crap! We are gentlemen. We are boys...dawgs. Why are we tripping?

The Meeting

OK, leave the name calling and the mamas out of this." Reluctantly, both Percy and Jalen back down and drop into their seats. Steve continues and says, "Can we please continue on with the meeting?"

Lawrence said, "Because, time is money and money is time. I don't have time for this foolishness. If it don't make money, it don't make sense; and this don't make any damn sense!" Jalen turns to Carmen, and said, "I need a drink, baby, some Hennessey VSOP, please." Percy said, "Yeah, and another bottle of <u>Cristal</u>, please."

Carmen rises to get their orders. Reverend Clayton said, "Drinking is not the answer…" Percy interrupts and said, "Rev., right now, I don't need a sermon, I need a drink! I let something out today that I've been hiding for so long. And I want to leave. But, I ain't ever run from anything; or anybody in my life but the police." The men pause as they take some time to settle down again.

Quickly, Steve changes the subject. He attempts to get the meeting back in order. Steve says, "Any new business?" Jalen said, "Let's take a break." Steve responds by saying, "No, we need to continue." Reverend Clayton agrees, "No, I'm in favor of a break, too!" Steve said, "Okay. FINE! I'm against it, but I guess you'll need some time now."

Shaking his head, Steve said, "This is a shame, this is business. We must leave our personal problems at the door. We won't get anything accomplished." Allen disagrees. Speaking up, Allen goes on to say, "No! This is the Black Men's Society! These are our problems. Problems, we face alone on a daily basis and must confront together. We're supposed to be there for each other. That is what we do. Never get it twisted, Steve!" After Allen finishes setting the record straight, Lawrence was in awe. Lawrence said, "Wow, Allen! Where did that come from, Superman!? There is no phone booth around, but you changed in a heartbeat."

Allen boldly says, "It says in our bylaws, we are here for each other; before money or personal gain. Teamwork is the common goal, which is sorely lacking in our race..."

That's when Allen notices Carmen walking across his line of vision. He follows her with his head. It seems she finally has a break in her workload. He's been thinking of how to approach her, and this break presents the perfect opportunity. Lawrence smirks as he notices Allen watching Carmen. Lawrence said, "Yeah, yeah, let's take that break." Allen walks over to Carmen at the bar. Reverend Clayton, Steve and Lawrence leave and walk outside for fresh air. Percy and Jalen stay at the table.

Chapter Three

Jalen & Percy

Jalen stares at Percy sitting across from him at the table. Percy said, "What the hell are you staring at?" Then Jalen said, "I don't really know." Percy could feel his blood start to boil. Percy said, "What the Hell does that mean? Then in a mimicking voice Percy said, *"I don't really know."*

Jalen took a deep breath. Then he said, "I can't figure you out. You're always ready to kick butt, but you like getting smacked on the butt!" Jalen glares at Percy in blatant disbelief. Percy was treating to smash his face in, and visibly growing angrier by the moment. Percy said, "Look here...I'm still a MAN and I'm going to kick your ass if you keep it up!" Jalen struggling to accept, what his ear have heard. He said, "You had it all... the women loved you and I looked up to you. Nobody messed with me out of fear of you, Percy. You were the enforcer of all of us...even the football team feared you." Percy begins nodding in agreement. He said, "I carried a gun then, too! He reminisces and throws his fists as if boxing. He continues to say, "My bronze wasn't bad either, but I was in jail and there were no guns. There are lots of crews in jail. It took more than one to get me, but they got me..."

He pauses. Then Percy slowly lowers and shakes his head.

Percy says, "How, could I go out into the world and pretend that I was heterosexual. I was raped repeatedly, more than seven times, man. It was like, how can I change my stripes and be a husband and father, knowing my past?"

Upon, hearing Percy's heartbreaking nightmare, Jalen finally understands. Now, he regrets his ill remarks toward Percy and the Rev. Jalen says, "I'm truly sorry, man."

Percy says, "Don't be. I put myself in that predicament. I sold dope. No rapper raps that part of the game; the consequences." Percy pauses, and then he looks off into the distance as he reflects on his past. Jalen said, "What can I do, man?" Percy said, "Use your gift. Tell my story, write about it! Put on paper the real side of selling drugs, going to jail and being out for money and self, but don't just tell the negative man. Show what real men are about, write of morals and integrity. We are losing our young black men and women every day to the lies. Rap songs and movies glorify a lifestyle that shouldn't be glorified. It's a death sentence."

Jalen begins waving his hand and dismissing the thought. Jalen says, "There's no money in that story. Besides, most people won't read it anyway; especially, the ones who need it the most. It's hard trying to get the truth published. It's unfortunate how rap, movies and the media can display only one side of that life. The truths about the consequences are seldom found in the telling, only in the living. Even, I can see there isn't any quality in that lifestyle."

Percy felt like he was talking to a brick wall, and could barely judge the distance of his words. Percy replied, "Everything can't be about the money. Some things have to be about love and caring. Blacks are still having children and they have dreams, too! The kids need to see the real nightmares out there; besides, If I could do it all over again. I would go to school, and become a business owner. I'd find a loving wife, and become a father, and simply be proud and prosperous!"

Jalen said, "What do you mean if...? You still can!" Percy pauses, shaking his head in denial. Then Percy said, "Yeah right...I've been tainted! I was the problem. Mothers sold everything to me from wedding rings, to their bodies, to their sons who would roll for me. I beat fathers for being $20 dollars short. I killed my black brothers and sisters with dope and violence. I'm damned to hell, and that's real! Then he sighs and drops his head. He goes on to say, "Although, I do repent every day, I ask God to forgive me daily. I don't know if this sinner's prayers are heard though. Jalen said, "I understand your pain, man...what made you tell us, anyway?" Percy hunched his shoulder and said, "I was a lot of things, but never a liar. You guys stand for what is right in my life. All of your realities are my dream. I just went about it the wrong way."

Jalen says, "I apologize for the remarks. Seriously, man, I didn't know and I'm truly sorry, my brother." Percy replied, "I said stop being sorry. I found someone that makes me feel good, mentally and physically. I've been shut down for many years. I haven't had sex in quite a while;

there's just too much pain to bear in my past. Hesitantly, Jalen, said, "So, you are not gay?" Percy responds, "I didn't say that; I had a couple of partners in jail, but I'm messed up." He points to his head. Then he said, "In jail I had no one to turn to, I was locked up for a long time. Hell, one week seems like a year in there and it gets pretty lonely. I just wanted someone to hold me. Outside life seemed so far away; muscles need tenderness, too."

Then Jalen admits, "I know that feeling. I can't get relationships right either. I'm cheating with every conversation that I have with another woman; especially, if she's fine." Percy gives him a quick 101 lesson in relationships. Percy said, "Man, fine is a dime a dozen; understand that. All that glitters, ain't gold. If you really want a relationship, you've got to listen to her to find out about her. Is she willing to share everything with you? Is she selfish or materialistic? She's got to have your back, and be willing to say when you guys are wrong. She's got to have your best interest at heart."

Jalen disagrees, "Most women can fool you, and they're good at trick ration. They just want the prize; a wedding ring. Man, they will go years waiting on that trophy! Giving you no lip service, cooking, and sexing you at the drop of a hat; but, listen to them on the phone talking to their girlfriends after a while. They always talking about leaving "don't give up the booty, girl." The other person is always ending every conversation with, "Girl, I would leave him if I was you." or "leave the baby, girl," "get his money girl," "I wouldn't cook that S.O.B. nothing girl!"

Jalen & Percy

Sometimes, I think she wants a girl, so I give her what she wants, HER GIRLS! See you when I see you, "girl."

Percy agrees, ""We must all grow up; women do throw themselves on men, but not all of them, just some. I know I don't want them, but they don't know that. They sometimes get naked quick. They feel rejected when I don't kiss 'em, rub on them, or fill their egos with "you cute, baby" and all that jazz. They want attention so bad. There are so many good women and so few good men. They always think there is another woman waiting in the shadows; more fine, or educated with more money, and most of all, freakier. Women go to clubs in the winter with halter tops on, waiting to get in a club. Then go to church with thongs on; with the little string showing. All the while, praying for a good man. They're even willing to steal a husband from another woman. Who doesn't know what she's got! If he's nice, with a business, or has a job with benefits; he's a keeper. Hey, mothers and fathers stopped instilling morals in their kids and teaching them the basics of decency a long time ago!"

In astonishment, Jalen wipes his forehead with his hand. Then he said, "Dang, Percy, where'd you learn all this?" Jalen thinks to himself, Man you should be the one writing a book. Percy said, "In jail, I read the Bible, Souls of Black Folks, The Final Call and Blackified. White people have always said, "If you want to hide something from a 'Nigga,' put it in a book." It took a prison sentence for me to read a sentence. I was so misguided back then. I would definitely do it differently; if I knew then what I know now. But, you can't go back. You can, however, share your knowledge with others in hope for a brighter future."

Jalen says, "I love you, bro, no matter what. Thanks for always being my big brother." Percy extends his hand to shake; and Jalen gave him a brotherly hug.

Percy smiled and said, "I love you too, man. And you'll find the perfect woman someday. You just have to be patient, and allow God to bring her to you. Now, let's get back to the others, and get this meeting finished."

Chapter Four

Steve, Lawrence & The Reverend Clayton

Steve, Lawrence and Reverend Clayton all stand outside, admiring the scenery of the Jazz club. Steve looks up and gazes at the beauty of the sunset.

Then Steve said, "It is a beautiful day, not a cloud in the sky. And, that breeze really feels good." Lawrence said, "Yeah, man, I can't wait to take these shoes off and kick back. Reverend Clayton said, "I've got the Youth Choir tonight. We need to practice for the Sunday Youth Extravaganza. So, my heels won't get any rest till about 11:30 or midnight tonight. Steve and Lawrence glance over at each other and both nod.

Silently, they both agree something must be said to the Reverend about his many activities. Lawrence exclaimed, "Rev., that's your problem. Where is the rest for you? Where's the quality time for family? You are with us doing Black Men's Society all afternoon. You will be at the church from seven till midnight. Not to mention, you've been out cleaning at the church daycare all morning. Come on, Rev. Something's got to give." Steve agrees, "That's right! You have to slow down, Rev."

Reverend Clayton exhaled deeply, and nods his head in agreement. The Rev. Says, "Yes, I do. I can't keep burning the candle at both ends, but..." Lawrence said, "Don't be going into the "15 Minutes before Church starts" mumbo. Save the sermon, this is us." The good Rev. says, "Watch it! I am still a man of God, so please don't bring the Father's way of life into this." Lawrence said, "Well, in your way of like, your wife should come first. She's a beautiful woman with needs and wants." Steve said, "Huh! She's spoiled and behaving like a Jezebel...a flat out TRAMP! Lawrence looks at Steve in disbelief at his audacity and rudeness.

Lawrence said, "No! What she is, is a woman without her man. She needs to be cared for. When was the last time you made sweet love to her in the daytime, or had a glass of wine with her?

Reverend Clayton said, "Last Sunday at church during the Lord's Supper; we shared a spot of wine with the congregation." Lawrence laughed and said, "Funny! That was with a thousand other members worshipping God!" Steve said, "Rev., I'm not going against God, but I'm going to pray for you. You're using your church to hide from your wife...yup. You really are. We all know it, and you do, too."

Then the Rev. said, "No, I am not! I love my wife with all my heart, she makes me whole. I've loved her since we met. I knew she would be my wife from the first smile, but

Steve, Lawrence & The Reverend Clayton

she's cheating on me! What am I supposed to do? Jesus!" Lawrence said, "Be a man about it! James, step up to the plate, stop thinking you're so damn perfect. You've made mistakes before. You are not God! You need guidance just like every-one else." Reverend Clayton said, "But, I am God's servant, I am here to lead the sheep. I'm an under shepherd, it's all I know. It's what I was called to do. I've known this from the time that I was a small child. Frankly, I don't know what else I can do."

Steve said, "Well, what's apparent is that you are not leading your woman right now! Rev. Clayton begins yelling. He said, "All right, Satan, enough of your BS!" Lawrence said, "Yeah, like I said, you a man, first!" Rev. Clayton said, "Forgive me Dear Lord. I cannot get so emotional and upset, I know better than that, Steve, but aren't you hitting a little below the belt, even for you?" Lawrence said, "What you need to ask is this: is your wife hitting someone below the belt? You better wake up man!" Your wife is out lying with someone else and you're just too scared to let her go. She's playing you for a fool and to add insult to injury, she's doing it in the comfort of the fancy cars you've provided for her! Damn!"

Rev. Clayton said, "I can forgive her; after all, it is my fault. So many things I wouldn't try, so many places I wouldn't go. He was on the verge of tears. Then the Rev. said, "Oh Lord...my soul is on fire! I need to be alone and pray." The Reverend walks a short distance away; he lowers his head and prays silently.

Steve grows angry and loud over the distress of the

Reverend's situation.

Steve turns to Lawrence and said, "All right Low, no more of this foolishness, can't you see he's already upset enough as is? He can't take any more of your BS. HELL, you want to ridicule him about being a real man and you can't even get an erection without the help of that little blue pill! You have no experience in this matter anyway. You'll probably never get married. You play with those young girls because a real woman wouldn't go for an educated fool using the Bar as a measuring stick for his manhood! See, that's your cop-out. You're always trying to bring someone else down to your level by stomping on their feelings. The Rev. has done more for his people than you ever will. He doesn't deserve this from her or you!

Lawrence said, "Steve… SHUT UP! You are just plain old wrong. I've made millions at the firm, people are rich because of me; and not all of them are white, either." Steve said, "Money isn't everything, Mr. "I don't want nothing old but my money." Besides, who likes your old butt? Those young girls who laugh behind your back; when you can't get it up? Or those white cats when you don't make partner at the firm….AGAIN? Even AFTER making them THEIR millions? Humph, where is your prestige? Where is your honor? Where is your woman who cooks for you and takes care of you when you're drunk and hung-over? All money isn't good money, bro. Didn't you learn that from the hood? Where's your dignity, family, kids, when was the last time you've even seen your grown daughters? What "Old Man" is sleeping with them, talking about that was some good young tender? Grow up, old man! Don't you know you get back what you put out?"

Lawrence lunges at Steve, and misses. The Reverend catches a fist trying to break them up. Reverend Clayton said, "STOP IT!! What is wrong with us; that we can't get the hood out of our system? You are too grown for this mess. Steve shakes the Reverend off him. Steve said, "No, let him go, it's time for him to pay the piper! Steve points his finger in the face at Lawrence. Steve said, "Your butt is mine! Lawrence looks at him like take your best shot! Then Lawrence said, "Hit my butt, and I will sue your black butt for everything you have. No Rev., let him go! I'll take a punch for a million, I am not scared."

Steve shakes head. Then he said, "It's like I said, where's your honor?" Lawrence grabs a ward of hundreds from his pocket. Then he said, "Jackson, Grant, Franklin and CLEVELAND; it's all about the money baby! Yeah, Cleveland, thousand dollar bills, baby. But, you don't know nothing about that!"

Reverend Clayton is still standing between the two of them. The Rev. said, ""I know we're better than this. We are a lot better than this." Then he sighs, and his shoulders begin to sag in defeat. The Rev. said, "I'll leave her Dear Lord, just please give me strength to hold this together. My Father God, please have mercy, stop this please. I'm sorry Lord...so very sorry, I'm sorry." Lawrence and Steve still look at each other with rage. Reverend Clayton notices he is bleeding from the mouth where he took the ill- placed punch. Fury is raging in Reverend Clayton, and he decides to back away from Steve and Lawrence.

Reverend Clayton had enough of his friend's foolishness. Finally, he said, "OK...F IT!! Do what you want! Kill each other, throw your lives away! Be what you so desperately; tried to get away from. Be killers and thieves, drunks, whores and drug addicts...and be against God! That's what you want, so be it. Give back all the houses, cars and the respect. Give it up! Give it up! Give up the Black Men's Society. Be a slave again. Let the people tell you when to rise, and when to sleep."

Steve replied, "I hear you, Rev., but this man believes words don't hurt. I'm going to give him what hurts and tell him about it! Rev. Clayton said, "You just don't get it, you guys are being foolish." Disappointedly, Lawrence said, "I'm too old for this. I'm going home. Steve, I never thought you were this petty and we called you a leader." REV. Clayton said, "To be honest, both of you are acting like children; talking about each other's lives. Instead of, complimenting on what each other has accomplished. You should have each other's back instead of trying to stab it. Stop using the name game to hurt one another. I thought we were beyond this kind of behavior. I thought I was dealing with black "MEN," not boys!"

Steve said, "Come on, Rev. He started it by trying to belittle you, and your family." Rev. Clayton said, "You did a good job of that, too! Shrugging his shoulders, Steve said, "What did I say?" Rev. Clayton said, "Huh... Jezebel and a flat out tramp," does that ring a bell? Come on, man, she's still my wife. Even though she's dead wrong...I love her. I know what she has done, but for now she is still Mrs. Clayton. God will give me the answer to deal with this." The Rev. points to Lawrence. "But for now, think about your friend Steve." Then the Rev. points to Steve. "And, think about your friend Lawrence." "You guys have beaten the odds."

The Rev. begins to chuckle and laugh. He said, "You all act like you're drunk off some Old English 800 or something." Steve smiles and says, "Lawrence man, don't leave. I messed up the meeting, my bag. We have a lot of important issues to still go over, and we really need your input." Lawrence smiled and said, "Man, I don't know?" Rev. Clayton looks at Lawrence and says, "Please stay, we have a lot to discuss. Come here, fellas, grab my hands. Dear Father, let our boldness be weak to the right frame of mind. Let our strength be about brotherhood, love and understanding. Let us build on character and morals that are in our souls. Let us be a family of brothers in our community, and stay focused on your word. Dear Lord, in Your Precious Son's name, Jesus Christ, Amen! Steve, Lawrence, and Reverend Clayton, all say, "Amen!" together. Lawrence pats the Rev. on the back. The said, "Thanks, Rev.! Now, let's do the right thing and get back to the meeting. We have a community to help."

Chapter Five

Carmen & Allen

Allen goes over to the bar; where Carmen is taking a break. Allen looks Carmen in her hazel brown eyes and asks, "May I have you to go?" She looks at Him and said, "No, you may not! Is this the real you? Humph, so Mr. Good Looking is a wolf in sheep's clothing, too, huh? Allen says, "No...No...I was just trying to be cool with a macho rough-neck kind of swag...you know? Don't women like that kind of stuff? Carmen crosses her arms and with attitude, said, "No, I don't know and "rough-neck" is a song that is really old and tired!" She turns, dismissing him from further conversation."

Allen said, "No, please forgive me, I was wrong. I'm trying to be someone I'm not." Carmen, "That was more like your friend over there...that seems to be his way of doing things. Kind of like a snake disguised as a butterfly... even though everyone knows it's really a snake! Allen said, "Who? Jaen?" Carmen says, "Yeah, I guess that's his name." Allen says, "No, I am not that way at all. I don't even have a steady girl, or a booty call for that matter. Right now, I'm a loner. Single." Carmen said, "Why is that?" She pauses. "Come on, you can tell me." Allen sees her boss come out from the back, and he looks over in her direction. Allen said, "Am I going to get you in trouble with your boss?" Carmen said, "Just answer the question? I'm on a break anyway. So, we have some time. By the way...thanks for being concerned, but I got this." She smiles and nods for him to continue. Carmen said, "Go ahead...answer the question, man. Allen chuckles. He says, "Well, I work a lot, and very hard. As a matter of fact, I have plans for my own company. But, it takes lots of cash to get it going. So, I have invested in myself. So, I don't have much time for women."

Carmen nods her head in understanding. She considers what he says.

Allen politely asks, "Are you so to the point all the time?" Carmen, "Most of the time, yes; so, why beat around the bush to get or give an answer? Although, you must think about your choice of words before they are spoken." Allen, "Do you ever make mistakes with fast answers? Where's the patience?" Carmen, "I usually know me. And, I know the things I like." Allen sheepishly, asks, "So, do you like me?" Carmen pauses, thinking. She said, "You seem like a gentleman, a little nervous, but a pleasurable person." Allen said, "What do you mean nervous?"

Carmen laughs softly. She jokes, "Oh, really nervous. I think you lack confidence. You're supposed to be oh-so-sure-of-yourself, Mister! Carmen reaches out and softly touches him briefly on the arm. Allen said, "I have confidence and I don't have time for confrontation. I'm just humble...but do you like me?"

Carmen said, "Okay, tell me three things you're looking

Soul Of A Man

for besides wealth. Do you read? Do you go to church?" Allen said, "First answer is: love, a solid foundation and a future. Second answer: yes, I read. I'm an electrician; I'd get burned up if I didn't. And, third answer: Yes, I go to church. Reverend Clayton is my pastor. I pay my tithes and volunteer. Now, quick, why do you like me?" Carmen stops smiling and looks him directly in his eyes. She said, "I like what I see and hear. And don't forget, I'm a quick thinker. As well as, a quick talker; Allen said, "Well, I'm slow like a turtle on a cold day...barely moving his feet. Ha, Ha." They both laugh at the image. Carmen said, "So, when is the last time you've been out?

Allen said, "Out like what? Club, cabaret, bar, play, what?"

Carmen said, "You know, out...out with a lady on your arm. A date." Allen said, "I'm embarrassed to admit it. It's been a good long time. I've been hurt before, and it took me a while to love myself more than I loved her." Carmen asks, "Why was that?"

Allen said, "I put her on a pedestal, and she didn't deserve to be there. But, I put her there anyway. I loved her. What can I say? I was sprung." Carmen said, "Wow! A man admitting he was taken by a woman!" Allen said, "Actually, it happens to a lot of us. We love to see our woman smile. We are the punks; when we are young. But, try to be the Casanovas when we're older. It's hard. So many women just want material things. And, a man just becomes a means to get it."

Carmen said, "That is not true. Okay, maybe with

some, but not all women are like that." Allen looks at her in disbelief. Carmen gently said, "No, really." Allen says, "Okay...why is it that when; women go out with their girlfriends, they share everything. But with their men, they think they deserve everything from picking her up, opening the doors, pulling out chairs, the movies, the food, the wine and the songs. With their girlfriends, everything is Dutch or they treat each other and she'll keep that girlfriend forever. But, on a date, they expect men to cater and cover it all. Don't they realize it takes two nowadays to make it? Things cost so much more than they used to. It's like they live in two different mind sets: the old days with men and the 21st Century with their girlfriends."

Then Carmen said, "In the past, men have played so many games. So, women are trying to catch up, I think." Allen said, "Like women haven't; they choose who they want between their thighs. A man can only give a resume; the woman gives out the job!" Carmen said, "We can also fire them!" Allen said, "But, if it were my company. I would do a thorough investigation; on who I would hire." Carmen said, "Hmmm...Do I detect some hostility?"

Allen's responds, "Yes, I'm a little hurt. I'm a good man. I work. I'm not the worst looking guy. I spend time with youth groups, attend church, I know how to treat a lady and I'm not scared to love again." Carmen said, "Then, why are you alone?" Allen said, "I see black women as beautiful but damaged. They want what shines from titles, Visa, Platinum, house and cars. They want "Fools' Gold." Women have always had the power. They used to like men of honor. But, now they like the guy on the corner; who risks his freedom and his life. A girl can look at him in a good light, selling dope to get a car, or a gold chain to look like he's something special. But, all he wants is the attention from her. So, he'll risk it all. Woman is the key to man. Think of how his rib protects his most vital organ: his heart. That's where she came from, his rib and she should continue to be the protector of his heart as well; that and his stomach." Carmen said, "So, you're trying to say God made a woman from a man's rib to protect his heart and stomach, and to feed him and find his heart through nourishing his soul with her love?"

Allen said, "Well, it's even better how you put it." Carmen leans back on her bar stool. Then she says, "But that's old fashioned!" Allen said, "What's wrong with old fashioned? There's nothing new under the sun. So, why is it that our people want change? But, don't know who we are changing from, or who we are changing into? Carmen nods. And she said, "You have a passion; I've never seen before. You present a fight for the right reasons. Wow, go on, black man!" Allen said, "Someone has to do it. We can't keep going backwards at home, in the office, in the community, nor in our state, and country." Carmen said, "You're right, baby. But, it's time to get back to work…and I thought you were shy. The strong, silent type…wow!"

Chapter Six

The Meeting Reconvenes

The men are returning to their seats while Carmen returns to work.

Steve said, "I hope everybody had enough time to clear their minds." Jalen said, "I had enough time to learn; we must have love for each other; most of all, ourselves."

Reverend Clayton said, "Amen! I really love you guys." Steve said, "By all means..."

Lawrence said, "Brothers, we have got to be strong for one another; even when we act like children, or worse, fools. We must be men and listen to each other's plans." Allen said, "We've come so far. Initially, we painted a picture of arrogance. We forgot our mission for the community, our society and our brethren."

Percy said, "Somehow, we let the past dictate the vision of tomorrow. We all grew up on the rough side, and we're still letting our past hold us back from greatness." Steve replied, "We are kings in our daily struggles. We must be objective when we talk about our community as a whole." Rev. Clayton said, "Where we need guidance, Dear Lord, we also need strength and togetherness. We need love of

Soul Of A Man

family and friends. We especially, need You, Dear Lord. We need Your blessings of hope, faith and love. We need You ever so dearly. We need Your protection, Your grace and mercy. We need You to humble us and for us not to try to do it alone as men. But to do it in Your Light. Let Your Will be done. Therefore, our efforts will be blessed. With Your love, we will not be shaken, and we shall not fail. We shall stand united as men in the name of Jesus, Amen."

Steve puts his hand on his chin and starts thinking. And he said, "Fellas, I think we need to ease away from community issues today or for at least right now. We need to move in the direction of brotherly love in the BMS. Jalen exclaimed, "What do you mean?" Steve said, "I mean, we need to understand; our membership as brothers." The others nod their heads. Rev. Clayton agrees, "I think that's a good idea, a very good idea." Lawrence disagrees. He said, "That's very time consuming."

Allen ignores Lawrence's remarks. Then he said, "No, it is not. We are, after all; our best investment. We need to get our priorities straight and figure out our goals and roles as men." Steve decides to take advantage of this unique opportunity.

Then Steve said, "Everybody will have a turn at having the floor. Speak your thoughts, your dreams, your ideas, and tell of your endeavors. Tell the truth about your life, relationships with your closest friends and relatives. We'll go in alphabetical order. Allen first, Reverend Clayton second. Next, come Jalen, then Lawrence, Percy, and I myself; last, but certainly not least." Allen said, "Why can't it be you first, Steve, since you're the chair, and all? The others nod in agreement." Steve said, "Okay, fine. I'll go first." Allen commented, "Naw man, I'm just giving you a hard time. I'm cool with going first." Lawrence said, "Get on with it, then. Tell your life story, man."

Allen says, "My name is Allen, most of you already know me. I'm my mother's middle child. I graduated top in my class, in everything and on every level. Reverend Clayton is my pastor. I like Italian food and the color blue."

Steve said, "Man, we know all of that, we don't need that kind of information. You spouted all of that off like you were going on one of those dating shows! We just want to hear your wants and needs out of life." Allen said, "Lawrence already told my life story. Percy said, "When did we start listening to Lawrence on anything, anyway?" They all laugh. Allen says, "Okay, then, well, I'm a hardworking man; who wants to be in love so very badly, but not with just anyone. I want children...a family of my own. I want a home. So, I can cook, clean and work on it, and show my children how to be responsible. Love my wife like there's no tomorrow. I want to grow old with her, and show my children what a real man is all about; mentally and physically. Show them my original role; as set forth by the Almighty Creator. I want to be a man of love."

Lawrence foolishly exclaimed, "Where's the money? Show me the money." Allen said, "Money doesn't make me happy; it makes me comfortable. Love also does that for me; it makes me comfortable. It relaxes me so very well, my soul will be at ease." Steve commented, "That's very honorable. If you have nothing further to add, we'll move on to Reverend Clayton." Reverend Clayton opens with, "I want God's blessing, His leadership ability. I want peace on Earth. I need and want my wife and my family. To give my soul harmony with love of Him, not material things; someone to make me whole. A future to change the community we live in; wherever that may lead us. To make children want to be kid again; to see the beauty in His blessings. It will be so bountiful. We will have all that was need to rejoice in Him. I want to be a great Under Shepherd; a great man. That's all, I want and need; next."

Then Jalen sadly confesses his heart and said, "I don't want to sleep around; I want a lady...just one lady. Someone that I can see eye to eye with; I want wealth and fame. I truly do, but most of all, I want and need respect from others. I want to know that I am on the right path. Dear Jesus, give me strength to be a better man; Lord, I have sinned. Forgive me Father, I want and need Your blessings." Lawrence is reluctant to come clean about the detail of his life. Then Lawrence said, "This is just getting too deep for me."

Reverend Clayton said, "Deep is to the soul. Let's keep right on the keeping on. Steve said, "Your turn, Low..." Lawrence said, "Okay, damn! You'll know me, why should I tell you how I feel?" Reverend Clayton said, "Because, we asked you to and because we care." Lawrence said, "OK, you want to hear it, here it is. I am hurting. I worry

The Meeting Reconvenes

myself to sleep most nights. I look at the firm; all the white partners and I know I'm the best person they have there. I still receive Christmas hams like everyone else. I make millions for that firm every year and still...no partnership. I win case after case. I drink the best, eat the best, I give a better effort than all the rest of them. I give it my all. I make more money; to say that I am better than you. See, I smile and dance for that firm. I'm "Ruthless Royalty" in the courtroom; but, a Jester in the office. I once was the token black, but now I am a valuable asset. I deserve better, damn it! I deserve better! Look at me, at the mercy of my black brothers. But, those egomaniacs hold me in contempt for simply wanting my due. In so many ways I am just like them. I look down on all; who look like me. My race and my color weigh so much; it is too heavy to bear at times. I am so confused, used, and exploited; that I...I dislike me and mine."

Steve said, "Welcome to the real world, Low. We must fight before we get to the ring. And we are losing the practice bouts. If you have nothing else to add, we can move on to Percy? No? Percy, it's your turn. Percy said, "Demons of the past got my mind, and they won't let go. Mistakes I've made keep reminding me of the fast life I have lived. How many homes I ripped apart? How many birthdays' fathers didn't come home to, because they were too busy getting' high in one of my crack houses. How many wives pawned their wedding rings for just one more hit? Young daughters licked their self- esteem; away turning tricks. How many boys I called "soldiers"; lost their lives for my cars, houses, cognac and MY money?! Now, look at me... the big sissy! Crying, repenting daily, knowing the people I've killed, and seeing the lives I've destroyed over, and over again in my head. Needing someone to hug. Only to find myself; in the arms of another man...THAT'S Hell. What can I say...I played the game and I lost. So...that's my dream? What a nightmare! You guys are all that's right in my life. Without you, I would probably kill myself just to get it over with. One bullet is all it would take." Then he held his head down; with the glimpse of a tear glistened in his eyes.

Reverend Clayton looks him in the eye. Then he said, "No son...don't talk like that. That's pure damnation and that's an unfair deal. Yes, we must play the hand out, but you must fight it, Percy. You can do it with God. God, help him...help him Lord. There's a brief moment of silence in honor of the plea for God's help.

Steve said, "Brothers, thank you for your honesty. Now, I'll gladly tell you about me. Well, growing up poor and being called ugly, I found out it's just a condition that only lasts if you allow it to. My goals have been just to wake up, and continue my thought from the day before; making it by being strong, and by being honest with myself. I've learned, and believe that it don't cost nothing to be fair. Being a leader is to be a hero. Stay calm when all else is in chaos. Malcolm and Martin were not without error but, the belief in a higher power brought about change for the betterment of our people and of them. So, I stay grounded in my belief that all men are created equal and that there

The Meeting Reconvenes

is only one God. I vow to do the best I can for my family and friends. By the way, I hope I'm blessed with a woman that has real love in her heart, soul and mind that equals my own. It gets lonely without a helpmate."

Reverend Clayton said, "That was beautiful, men. We are finally getting to know each other as men. I've learned so much today. I vowed to the Man upstairs I will talk to the congregation about getting an Assistant Pastor to help with the growth of the church. Then, I can delegate some of my duties. Perhaps with some counseling, my wife and I can make our marriage work. I owe her that much. I am so proud that I have friends like you guys."

Steve smiles and said, "you'll made me so proud, like it is finally time to fight as a whole for our community, to see the light of love in our neighborhoods. It is also, time for me to settle down, not be so hard on women; who care about me; so, that I can have a real loving relationship."

Percy listens and his spirit is uplifted. Percy said, "Yeah, it does feel good to get all of this off my chest. I really felt like quitting, so many times...fighting such a battle can get lonely. Lying to whoever, comes near me is tiring. I am glad that I have my brothers. The same sun that shines in the suburbs, well, it shines in the ghetto, too. God can make the blind see, and I know He can make a man out of me!

Lawrence said, "Well, I'm going to work on changing my way of thinking. It's time for me to learn some new tricks. I am an old dog, but I'm ready to learn how not to be so judgmental and arrogant. I'm going to learn how to really listen to whomever is speaking. I am sincerely trying to be a better man; in trying to understand that all people have issues. I promise to fight for their right to be heard; if they can't fight for themselves. Somehow, I will get my own firm, and be my people's best friend. Santa Claus is coming straight to the ghetto! Jaen said, "I'm going to write for my young brothers. Talk about the ballers, the hustlers, and the loser who steals young minds in exchange for the devils bidding to be done. We don't need any more babies having babies, crack deals in the high schools and city streets. No more fighting in the streets over territory; that has nothing but abandoned buildings, burnt out houses and stores, trees that don't grow, and cars left behind for the scrap heap. I am going to write for my people to be heard; for equality and quality of life; and the nourishment of dreams! Carmen walks over to the table to see if the guys are finished.

Carmen said, "Excuse me gentlemen; is there anything else that I can get for you?" Allen said, "Yes lady, I want your number, address, a date on Friday, and a bottle of chilled champagne for my brothers in celebration of coming together as men. Carmen said, "Okay, yes to everything you just asked for. She smiles and walks away to get the champagne. Allen smiles from ear to ear. Allen said, "I'm proud, happy and I'm comfortable. I am feeling blissful." Hallelujah! Lord have mercy. This is what the BMS is all about; picking up your brother, when he can't pick himself up; to be a team and realize a dream; to be one with God and His children. Hallelujah!"

Steve said, "This meeting has come to an end for us,

The Meeting Reconvenes

Brothers. If there are no questions or other disclosures. May we always stay black and true to our God, family and friends. Together, we say Black Men!" Everyone said, "Black Men!" All the Brothers disburse from the meeting at Baker's Keyboard Lounge.

Chapter Seven

Reverend Clayton's Home

Reverend Clayton quickly drives home to see Rose, his wife. When Reverend Clayton arrives home and enters the bedroom to confront Rose about her infidelity, he sits on the bed as Rose enters the room. Rose said, "Hi Dear how was your meeting?"

The Rev. says, "Most interesting meeting we've had yet, I witnessed something rare today. A good man sometimes hits a snag too. We need the company of good brothers to release some of the fears, pain and stress we deal with in life; yeah, rare indeed." Rose said, "Sounds like you guys had a good old heart to heart. The men's version of "Exhaling!" Praise God!"

Rev. Clayton begins to speak with conviction in his voice; he said, "Always praise God, and God won't allow you to be played for a fool, no matter the circumstances. Not, if you truly believe in Him. Rose stops what she's doing and turns to face him, sounding guilty. Rose gets an attitude. She says, "What do you mean? Reverend Clayton said, "Come on now Rose! I know and you know! What's done in the dark will always come to light. You've been

Reverend Clayton's Home

fooling around on me Rose; now tell me I'm lying?!?! Rose gets defensive. She said, "What the hell are you talking about, James?" Rev. Clayton said, "I have thousands of members in the congregation, Rose. Do you really think Toledo is that far, 60Miles?!?! Are you crazy, dumb or you just didn't know any better, which is it? Never mind. By the way, camera phones take pretty good video. I saw you with my own two eyes going into a motel with a man; who wasn't me! Not a picture Rose, VIDEO. You had on the coat that I just bought you! How could you?!?! Have you no shame!? Rose sits silently for a moment, thinking if this is the time to deny his allegations, or tell him the truth. She opts for the truth.

Rose defiantly said, "Look James, I am sorry you had to see that. But, damn it! I'm human...I need tenderness too. I need a man's touch. All these years I've had to share you with thousands of people, "will you pray for me Reverend, help me Reverend, I lost my job Reverend, baptize my ugly conceived in sin baby Reverend"...well Reverend, who's been praying for me?!?! My man is gone on a daily basis and I am left alone and lonely. What am I supposed to do; watch Tyler Perry movies by myself all day long?" I'm bored and hurting...all by My Lonesome. Reverend and when you do finally get home at night, you are too tired to make love to me. You don't even touch me most nights. Then you're gone first thing in the morning. Then, to add insult to injury, you send me out with the "Lady Folk" of Reverend Clayton's big ole' church; the old biddies back stab and lie on and to me every chance they get. Stabbing me with their words! Rose begins whispering in a mocking tone. "Here she comes, be quiet girl... The tone in his voice gets louder. Ooo, you look so nice, First Lady...I made you a cake, First Lady!" They all know I'm First Lady in name only! I'm fed up to here with it, with them and with you!

Rev. Clayton said, "That's my anointing, Jesus called me to preach.

Rose said, "Well, preach to your congregation while another man makes me scream for sweet Jesus! You touch with your words...humph; I need another kind of touch."

Rev. Clayton is on the brink of insanity; and he yells, "Oh God!! She is going to make me lose my mind up in here...Dear Lord, the devil is trying to make me touch her right now...Satan, I rebuke you, get thee behind me!!!" Rose backs up as, he stomps towards her. He threw her on the bed. Then the Rev. said, "One, two, three...Jesus, give me strength! I am more of a man than you know... devil, I rebuke you, and I rebuke you, I REBUKE YOU!!!

Rose struggles, but breaks free from his grasp. She says, "That's right, pray. Pray for me too! You pray for everyone else in the world!" Rev. Clayton said, "Well, I've been doing that ever since I met you." In a matter-of-factly tone of voice, Rose says, "Look James, I love you madly, but for years I've sat around waiting. I am by your side at funerals. How many funerals can you do in a year anyway? Hmmm, seems like I'm waiting on death just to get next to you. I'm living in a lonely, Hell!"

Rev. Clayton belligerently said, "Baby girl, it's my duty

to the church and to the Lord." Rose said, "James, what about your duty to me, you know, forsaking all others? I'm tired of eating fried chicken, spaghetti and string beans every Sunday. We are either in the Fellowship Hall at the Church or at some member's house...half of them can't even cook!" Rev. Clayton said, "I'm a man of God, Rose, and proud to be such. Lord knows I love you more than life itself, but don't make me choose between you and God. Baby, you will lose every time. I'll miss you... but you will lose." Rose said, "Then we lost each other a long, long time ago!" On the brink of tears; they sadly go their separate ways.

Chapter Eight
Coming Together

Allen and Carmen are on a date at Belle Isle Park. It's only been four short days; but they feel as though they have known each other for timeless Centuries. One look pierced his soul; he admits that he had never felt so deeply for a lady. As, Allen stared into Carmen's big beautiful hypnotic eyes; her eyes connected her to his soul.

Allen boldly said, "Sweetheart, God gave me an early Christmas gift, and I am so happy that it's you. You are what I've been in need of; a friend who understands my heart. Carmen said, "I'm Flatterer! Are you sure it's not Casanova that dwells within? Allen said, "No, baby, I'm just being honest. Maybe there's a little bit of a Don Juan lurking in there somewhere, but mostly it's just a man who is falling in love."

Carmen's said, "Wow Allen, did I hear you right? Please don't play with my heart, it's fragile. I am so used to doing it alone, and I don't need another man playing childish games. I don't have the time, or the patience."

He says, "There's no time limit on love. I listened to

your heart, and I watch your actions. I see the kindness in your eyes, and I feel it in your spirit. You wanting to be a nurse, caring for those that cannot care for themselves, wow, now that's what I call honorable."

Carmen, "Well, truth be told, I feel the same way about you. I see the kind of man you are. You truly are a rare find, as very compassionate, hardworking, and beautiful as the autumn leaves. You make a woman want to believe in love again. Allen points to her heart. Allen said, "Are you sure there's no Jill Scott in there; because that makes my soul smile." They sweetly embrace with a kiss.

Diner On The East Side Of Detroit—Mid Afternoon

Now, it's midafternoon, and Percy gets a call from his mother G-Mama, as she's referred to by friends and family. Her real name is Grace. She has a lot on her mind, and wishes to speak with her son face to face. Percy is eating lunch at a Diner on the east side of Detroit.

Percy answers the phone. He said, "Hey Mama, how you doing'? G-Mama said, "Boy, you eat today? You're looking as little as a, child." Percy sighs. He said, "I just finished eating, Mama." G-Mama said, Then why the sad face, baby? Tell Mama what's wrong." Percy said, "Nothing's wrong, Mama."

G-Mama could hear the sadness in her baby's voice. She concernedly said, "One of them hot tailed girls done played with your mind again? You know you can't buy love. Haven't you learned that yet? Quiet as it's kept, all money isn't good money neither...especially when you done wrong to get it. Wrong is wrong, no matter what! Percy said, "Well, money isn't the problem, Mama. The ends are meeting...sugar bread baby!" G-Mama said, "Don't talk to me with that slang! So, if money isn't the problem and it isn't one of those trashy girls you be messing with. Why the long face? Ahh, don't tell me nothing's wrong, a mother knows when something is wrong with her child; no matter how grown he thinks he is. Did you really think that I didn't know all those years; when you were peddling that poison to our people? You're so head strong boy...just like your father. You'll were just alike, you two." She begins shaking head in amazement. "Humph, no one could tell you two anything. One wants to walk with the Lord, the other with the devil. God bless his soul. He was such a loving man, a peace maker. But, he would never back down."

Sadly, Percy said, "Yeah, it got him killed trying to stop a fight between two street hustlers; who didn't care about nothing!" G-Mama said, "But your father did. You know his favorite saying was, "Why send a man down a tunnel with a train coming, and the lights is off?" Percy said, "Well, why didn't he see that train with the lights off? G- Mama said, "They were young boys like you; you had all of your father's teachings. Why didn't you apply that to your life? Percy said, "I did, I didn't back down! G-Mama said, "Where did it get you? Jail for...for years, for some shiny trinkets, cars, houses, money?!?! You wouldn't listen either."

Coming Together

Percy said, "Come on Mama, I don't need this! Daddy left me to fend for myself, and I did." G-Mama said, "He left you money for college. You wanted to sell drugs for money and street respect. For, 10 years and what did it get you? 10 YEARS IN A JAIL CELL! No amount of money can get that time back. You were taught better. A year has four seasons; every year you lost four times 10. Forty seasons of living, and I can bet my world on it: you were dying in a cage, because nothing grows on cement." Percy said, "I paid my dues."

G-Mama said, "To whom? What lies have you been listening to? All your life for a Rap song from Biggie to Pac. Yeah, kids rapping about dead fold. "Live by the sword, die by the sword." Holla, if ya hear me....while they wake up in a jail or never wake up at all!" Percy said, "Mama, I don't do it no more. That's their fault now. Not mine." G-Mama said, "Where are my grandchildren for me to be proud of? All I got is you and you're not like your father. Why can't you change? Undo your damnation! I'm the one who led you...this is my fault."

Percy said, "No Mama! No Mama, I'm sorry...I'm trying so hard. I'm really am trying. I just feel like my soul is bound for Hell. G-Mama said, "Oh baby, those 10 years; I prayed that I would see you again. After losing your daddy, I never thought I would lose you in this lifetime. It's been so hard. Percy is almost brought to tears. He said, "I know, I know Mama. If I could do it all over again, I would be a better man." G-Mama said, "My day began with prayer, ended with prayer and all nine months and in between, was prayer filled. Twenty-seven hours of labor before your first day of life. What can I do but pray? That's all I know." Percy said, "Why talk today? Life is hard enough now. Not today." G-Mama said, "Life is life. Always do what's best for God to have favor on your soul." Percy said, "You said it all the time, Mama, "Do what's best." I didn't listen and it has been rough."

G-Mama reassures him; and she replies, "Baby, I don't know your past and I'm scared to ask. I know you're troubled and no matter what it is, I'm going to love you. You are my child, you know that don't you? That, I'll love you no matter what."

Percy went on to repent and say, "Mama, I love you too. I'm sorry, Lord, I'm sorry. Mama, you were right; a hard head does make a soft behind." His mother reaffirms his faith in the Lord. G-Mama said, "Just pray. Pray baby. Pray hard. God is a forgiving God. But, you must mean it. God knows what's in your heart."

Percy said, "Dear Lord, my life has been full of sin; I want to be a better man. I know I can't do it alone. I need You. I'm tired. Talk to me, Lord. Let my soul be free to do what's right, Father. I want to, no, I need to follow in Your spirit, Father." G-Mama said, "Let it out, baby. Talk to Him every minute, every hour. Ask for forgiveness, He'll work it out. Lay all your burdens down at His feet. Percy, do it right now. You can't bring back yesterday, but today and tomorrow you can make a change for the better. Don't back down this time, stay in God's light and do what's right. He'll see you through it, just believe, baby.

I'm tired now. I need to go home and rest." Percy, listen this time. Percy said, "Yes, Mama, I will."

Reverend Clayton's Home— Several Mornings Later

Reverend Clayton has moved out of the bedroom, but only to the adjoining suite on the other said of the bathroom. He and Rose still follow the same bathroom routine as before. He's up first and showers, then it's Rose's turn. This repeats for several mornings and there's a montage of their morning routine.

One early morning, Rose and Reverend Clayton both walk into the bathroom at the same time. It's about 4AM. Rose is wearing the sexy gown; he bought her for their last anniversary. He's wearing the Christmas boxers she bought him two years ago with the snow-women on them. They both stop and longingly look at one another for the first time in a long time. Rose and Reverend Clayton say, "I'm sorry...I miss you...I love you. They run to each other and hug and kiss. They hold each other for a while. Reverend Clayton walks her to his adjoining room.

Rev. Clayton said, "We need to talk. You know I love you, don't you, Rose? Rose said, "Yes, I know but James, I can't go on like this. It's just too much. Maybe, not for you, but for me, it's simply too much to bare. I didn't ask for it, I didn't ask to be a preacher's wife...to walk a narrow line. That was your calling...and I love you for it. You are the most decent man I've ever met. You've treated me like royalty, like the father I never had. You spoiled me with your kindness, but I'd rather have you...all to myself. Forgive me, Lord for being selfish. Damn the rest...they are stealing my joy, my man, my husband!"

Rev. Clayton said, "Rose... why have you never mentioned these feelings to me before? I am a Reverend, not a mind reader." Rose said, "I see the passion, the conviction, and the honor in what you are called to do. I see the joy it brings you to help others. I see so many women come to the church, lonely, wanting, needing and praying for a good man; and I have the greatest man of all. How can I steal your joy? However, I'm losing myself in your world. I love you, James. I know I made a mistake in judgment, and I don't know how to correct it. Sometimes, I sit and pity my circumstances. Instead of correcting; the wrong I've done. I am not you, James; God didn't give me a heart like yours. You can share your world with so many until you have no time for yourself." Rev. Clayton said, "I understand, Rose, I understand... now." Rose said, "Can you ever forgive me? I am so very sorry; that I sinned against God's commandments, and that I've shamed my husband. I am sorry, James."

Rev. Clayton said, "Only Jesus knows your heart. My Uncle Rather always said, "It ain't no fun when the rabbits got the gun!" I thought you would always be Here, as my best friend, my soul mate, my wife, my angel from God. Rose... Rose... Rose...my flower. I do love you." Rose said, "Why is your heart so beautiful?"

The Rev. said, "My Rose." He pauses. "Let us pray together." They both bow their heads. Then he said, "May

Coming Together

God keep us together, may He bless our family, home and church. Dear Lord, we humble ourselves in your presence, and beg for your sweet mercy. Lord, strengthen our relationship and make our hearts pure and tender towards one another. Let us not be bound with unforgiving and undeserving hearts. You gave Your only begotten Son for our sins, so that we may have everlasting life. Cleanse us of our sins against You, and each other. Lead us, oh Lord, in the ways we should go. Let us forgive and move on with love, life, and determination to be living witnesses to Your greatness, Your goodness and Your blessings. Amen." Rose says, "Amen."

Chapter Nine

Redemption

It's a new day, and it also brings life's challenges and tragedies. The setting is right outside Highland Park Community High School. We see a young lady with bruises on her face outside the high school. She's been hanging with the wrong crowd. She digs the ballers, because of the street power and respect. She ends up being physically abused by one of the hustlers; and a young man who likes her; now thinks he is her protector. He's now seeking revenge.

The young lady is talking to the young gentleman. She said, "Don't, leave him alone! He isn't worth it; don't mess up your life for trash! The young man said, "He's goanna pay. He had no right to touch you. Now, I'm going to touch him!" He lifts his shirt; to show her the gun in his waistband. As, they both proceed to walk to the auditorium.

Auditorium Of Highland Park Community High School

The Black Men's Society are attending the "Alumni Day" Rally; in the high school auditorium. Students and staff are present. Steve turns to speak to the guys. He says,

Redemption

"This is a good idea, this brings back some good memories. Lawrence said, "Yeah, this is nice. Funny, I could not wait to leave here twenty years ago, and now I'm actually proud to be back." Reverend Clayton said, "I am so glad to be a part of this, directing young souls, guiding them into adulthood. What a blessing it is take part in the molding of their lives." Lawrence nods in agreement, and said, "Yeah, always reaching and teaching, I guess that's your job. Get your check Rev., but know that these are difficult times. Steve said, "Right, right, right, I haven't been here in about ten years myself. The children are more than coldhearted. What happened?"

Lawrence said, "They are full of chaos; they can destroy something so quickly; bathrooms have no dividers or toilet paper dispensers, wow." Steve said, "No home training, no fathers. But, that's why we're here: to give back from whence we came! We have to show them how important alumni are to our community."

Reverend Clayton said, "That is the best idea yet! I am full of joy right now; hmmm, whose idea was this anyway?" Lawrence said, "Jalen, who is not here at the moment." Steve said, "Jalen is changing, he's getting wiser; one day at a time. I see the difference in him." Lawrence replies, "He's always had good ideas; some of his writings and poetry pieces will make you think. He's a very deep brother, but still chasing that almighty dollar and women."

Rev. Clayton said, "Love will corner his heart one day. Money will be there for the making, but love? Love is just slow and kind and it will reveal the promises of God. Jalen cares, he really does, give him time." Lawrence said, "He does?!?! He's got money, and fame on the brain. But, who am I to talk? It reveals me at times too."

Steve said, "It RUNS you, man! It is your god!" Jalen and Allen arrive.

Jalen walks up. He says, "What up, HP!?" Allen said, "Who dat talking about beating those Parkers!? Lawrence said, "What up, baby boy?" The Rev. said, "Hey guys, it's good to see you gentlemen. Jalen, great program, I mean that. I wish it were more of this in the community. Just what the doctor ordered." Steve said, "Jaybird, you out done yourself, man. I'm proud of you." Allen said, "This is cool brother. Man, I always wanted to be a science teacher, to show my love every day to the children. I'm proud to be here too; it beats being a statistic." Jalen said, "you'll try to make a brother cry?" Rev. Clayton said, "Where's Percy?" Jalen said, "He'll never set foot in this school again." Rev. Clayton said, "Oh yes. His father was killed outside picking him up you know. I can't blame him." Steve said, "That's a hard pill to swallow. I guess it has to be just the Fab HP Five then." Allen said, "Yeah, I guess." Principal Calita Pettway comes over to the men.

Principle Pettway says, "Gentlemen, thanks. Thank you for your kindness, strength, love and support. It is a tremendous thing to give of yourselves to these children. They need good men to step up to the plate. Sisters cannot and should not have to do it alone. The ratio is 85% female teachers to 90% single moms at home. Bottom line, we need more men, we need you guys."

Steve said, "Yeah, we are ready. It's time for a change. Then Rev. Clayton said, "Amen. We can't just teach from the pulpit; it's time to attack the streets, schools and homes. Mrs. Pettway said, "What do you need?" Steve said, "Just the podium and the mic." Rev. Clayton said, "Let us pray." Lawrence commented, "Let's say it silently and quickly. I don't have that much time."

Allen shakes his head at Lawrence. Allen said, "One day, you will believe in a moment of prayer for the Most High." Lawrence shrugs shoulders. Then he said, "I'm just talking to a bunch of kids. Rev., Allen, dang, you all ALWAYS praying." Looking at him; Allen said, "Suit yourself." Lawrence said, "I don't have time."

Principle Carlita Pettway addresses the large auditorium filled with youngsters. She puts her hand up in order to silence them. The principle turns to the men. Then she said, "Now, now gentlemen. In this life, I've learned that you must always make time for God. Only the Lord knows when or worse, IF you will get a second chance to talk to him from this side of heaven. One should never be too tired, busy, or think one is too important to have a talk with God."

Lawrence said, "Come on!! Not you too! I'm a sinner, okay, everybody?! Woooooo, now say a silent prayer, please! Lawrence mumbles, "Wow." The Principle shakes head in disbelief. Oh, he'll learn; God has a way of teaching old dogs new tricks. She chuckles.

First to address the podium is Steve. He said, "Good morning, Parkers. I thank God for this blessing, to be able to speak with you this day. You remind me of so many of my friends. You look like them, but I know you are not them. Your smiles light up this room, just as theirs did twenty years ago. Youth with dreams; it's a beautiful thing. Some succeeded and some did not live long enough; to see their dreams become a reality.

I wouldn't trade my life for anyone else's. Not even with the man; who was born with the Silver Spoon in his mouth. Why? Because, God gave me purpose that was meant just for me. I was made to be a strong man, one who walks with integrity and is filled with morals and love. That is the gold in life, and it will shine forever more.

One of the teenagers said, "Give me some of that gold, so I can pawn it for some paper! Principle Carlita Pettway walks up to the microphone. She said, "All right, quiet down, or risk receiving suspension, or detention. Homeroom teachers, please take down the names of any disorderly, and rude students. Black Men's Society, please continue."

Steve said, "Rules: you can be a trend-setter, or the jokester. The choice is yours and yours alone. It's a cold, cold world. Millions of young and old men make poor choices and they end up sitting in prison; waiting to be told when to shower, eat, sleep, heck, even when to use the bathroom. Now is the time for you to make smart choices, make your own choices. Do it before someone else makes the choice for you. Wake up! Mama, Daddy and Uncle Ray-Ray can't hold your hand forever. No one, but you are in control of your destiny. Beat the odds; your friends can't do it for you. Set your goals and strive to achieve them. You must have a mind-set to be a leader; and not a follower. Your friends can give you all kinds of excuses; when you go to jail." I couldn't call, or come see you like that, locked up like a dog." He changes his voice, "Man, it was too hard, you know dawg?" Yeah, right, he was with your girl the moment they slammed the door behind you. He didn't have time to write, because he was too busy kickin' it with the crew. That's why I'm here to tell you, get your education. Learn a trade, own your own business. Become something greater than what you already are. You are descendants of Kings and Queens. Don't destroy your dreams, or allow anyone else to have the power to do so. Bring Jalen, one of the toughest writers around to the stage please. He's here to share his experiences with you. Be encouraged, young folks."

Jalen addresses the crowd. He says, "What's up HP?!?! I am quite honored to be here with you guys today. I come from the streets; many of you are from the same place. But, I am here to tell you; that there is more to life than these streets. I wouldn't be the man that I am today; if I did not have a strong foundation. And, for me, it began here, right here in HP. These walls have so many fond memories and some hard times too. I am not going to mislead anybody; it's rough and yes, sometimes it hard to do the right thing; rather easy to do wrong. Remember your legacy will be built on the right that you do now; or the wrong. Martin Luther King, Jr. and others' legacies are being honored by the simple freedoms that we enjoy this day. But, sometimes take for granted. Most of us are too young to remember how hard it was for our people. There was a time when we could not vote, sit at the counter in a diner, sit in the front section of a public bus, go to a hospital, decent school or even read! We were not "allowed" to look a white man directly in his eyes. Our elders shed blood, sweat, and tears. Some even gave their lives for us. We owe them much more than what we've been giving. Give back by using your five senses that God gave you. Please use those precious gifts. They command respect. Those are your weapons of survival. Believe in God, He's real and believe in yourselves; "To thine own self be true."

Carlita Pettway makes her way to the microphone. Mrs. Pettway said, "You see there is nothing wrong with showing compassion towards your fellow man. It brings tears to my eyes to see these strong men giving their hearts to you young folks; to show you a side that is rarely spoken about. Black men and our history; President Obama made history. Dr. Anderson made history with the personal computer; Garret Morgan to this day makes the world stop...you children. You have a chance to make history of your own. Please take heed to these words of wisdom that we are sharing with you today. You can never say no one ever told you. Proudly carry the message like it is your sword, and shield and be proud of where you come from. Now, coming to the stage is Allen of BMS. A teenage girl says, "He's fine! Oooo wee, girls, he is fine!"

Allen said, "I'm not much of a talker, but thanks for having me. I just have this to say, "Do your best, stand up for the ones that cannot stand up for themselves. Follow your dreams, because they are yours. Thank you…peace, love and light."

Rev. Clayton said, "You're next, Lawrence." Lawrence said, "Man, you'll don't need me. You'll doing a good job." All the guys and Ms. Pettway look at Lawrence, silently saying, "Come on, now." Lawrence said, "Okay, dang, I'll do it." Principle Pettway said, "Well, that was strong, sweet and short. Now, we have Mr. Lawrence Burgess coming to the stage."

Lawrence foolishly addresses the youngsters. He smiles and said, "Thanks a million, I mean a million because I want to be rich, not just secure, but really wealthy. A step beyond rich…why? Because, I have two degrees and that was my only way of getting out of the ghetto. See, I felt that I was better than that, and I am…" His words trail off as a commotion occurs behind them on stage.

A young man runs past Reverend Clayton, and bumps into Lawrence. Another young man with the gun runs in. The youngster with the gun yelled, "I'm going to get you, punk!" He fires two shots from the gun, striking Lawrence in the leg, and hitting the other young man in the chest. Both, of them fall to the stage. Lawrence crawls over to the boy to assist him.

Lawrence yells, "Don't die on me!" Students and faculty run screaming!!!! Lawrence puts his arms about the boy and calls out for help. Lawrence yells, "Call 911! Someone help me…please, help me…please, Jesus, please, somebody help!"

Blood oozes out of the boy's almost lifeless body; as he lays there in a fetal position. Reverend Clayton tackles the shooter, who just stands there looking paralyzed with shock. Reverend Clayton tackles the shooter, who just stands there looking paralyzed with shock. Principle Pettway said, "I told him he's need Jesus on this job!" Allen holds a group of students back...as sirens sound!

Sunday Morning—Reverend Clayton's Church

Early, that Sunday morning, Reverend Clayton and the men walk up to the doors of the church. Carmen and Rose sit in the pews, worshipping together.

Rev. Clayton sits next to Allen, Percy, Steve, and Lawrence. The Rev. turns to Allen. Rev. Clayton said, "This is the first Sunday, that I have not delivered a sermon in the past four years; sun, rain, sleet or snow. God don't take holidays, so why should I? However, I've found that I am not as good as God; I'm just a man."

Allen said, "You are a beautiful man, just as you are Rev., God doesn't make any mistakes." Steve agreed, "Right Rev., take that pressure off of your back. Listen to the word. It will all change for the better, just hold on." Allen looks at Carmen. Then he turns to the men and says, "I'm ready to jump and should for joy! This is a beautiful day. You'll, I got my girl, my boys and I'm in the house of worship. What more could I ask for?" Lawrence said, "It is a beautiful day indeed. I have a lot to be thankful for, too. I am more than willing to give God His just due.

Once upon a time, I didn't have time for God, but after watching how HE spared that young man's life and healed my body; I now know that God is real. I'm ready to praise Him, fellas, because He knows how to get your attention!"

Reverend Kinlock, the newly hired assistant pastor delivers his '**Sermon on Forgiveness.**' At that moment, Percy walks through the door and secretly sits in the church hallway. The sermon convicts his soul. Percy's repenting heart deeply longs for redemption. He eventually drops to his knees and talks to God.

Percy with tears running down his face cried out unto the Lord. He confessed, "God, forgive me. For, I have sinned against You. I was lost and couldn't see You. These burdens have corrupted my life. Now, I need You to be my leader; the head of my life. I'm sorry, dear Lord, Mama, Daddy, I didn't mean to let you down, please forgive me, forgive me."

Percy burst into the church and falls to his knees at the altar. He says, "I'm sorry, dear Lord, forgive me Jesus. Forgive me cleanse my soul, Lord, do it for me!"

The Black Men's Society runs out to Percy with open arms. They all hug him with tears in their eyes. Allen said, "Let it go, let it go. It's alright, **Brother**."

FADE TO BLACK

Falling in love in 30 Days

Falling in love in 30 Days

May 27, 2010 – 3:33am

Phantom pieces.
Love quest.
Everything I can do.
I will do for you.
Big things and little ones, too.
My love honey,
Won't be sweet enough.
It's strait up sugar cane.
I just want to please you.
I'm doing my best.
For, you my love,
My friend, my woman.

               Luv R3

To every woman that needs a loving man. Need it and achieve it!

May 28, 2010 – 10:32pm

I searched no more.
I found someone,
That I adore.
She moves me.
She sets my words free.
She belongs to me.
I am hers'.
No more games to play.
It's love.

She is whom, I'm thinking of.
Let me write a love story.
Now, I can treat a woman
Like a Lady.

Luv R3

May 29, 2010 – 3:49am

Careless Whispers,
But I roar.
She's the one that I adore.
For, her happiness
I must do more.
Laughter and song,
She feels that she belongs.
With me for eternity,
My precious jewel.* this is for my new Woman I
shall write to her,
POETRY;
about how she makes me feel.
This is a test of my patience,
And commitment to a goal,
To Honor her.

Luv R3

May 30, 2010 – 2:10am

A day with you is like springtime,
With no rain.
But, if it rain,
I expect it.
And I treasure every drop.

For, everything grows,
Like our love.
You are my ultimate flower.
You are not like the rose,
Or bird of Paradise.
You are the greatest flower,
Rain on me!
I need sunlight, rain,
And **YOU**.

Luv R3

May 31, 2010 – 7:00am

You scream deeper and deeper.
So, I went hold nothing back.
I gave it my all.
And it pierced your soul,
I've never gone so deep.
As, I stared into your beautiful hypnotic eyes,
those eyes connected me to your soul.
I found out where your love lived,
Through your beautiful eyes.
Now, I dwell there with you.

Luv R3

June 1, 2010 – 2:39am

Soulful wonder.
Extreme to bear witness,
to Passion.
A deep desire that cannot be contained,
by mere mortals.

As I taste your lips,
And massage your hips,
There's nothing like my
Wonder Woman.
For, I got to be her
SUPERMAN!

                                        Luv R3

June 1, 2010 – 11:18pm

On our weekend off,
As you were falling
Into a sleep slumber,
I caressed your temples,
and sang a soft lullaby.
I watched you ever so proudly.
Rubbing the small of your back,
Kissing your eyelids,
Wishing I were in your dreams.
Kissing your every finger,
And at that moment,
I knew you were
My Obsession!

                                        Luv R3

June 1, 2010 – 12:49pm

Insatiable,
No matter how many times
I kiss you,
I want a million more.
No matter, how much I touch you,

I need it again.
Your body, is my best friend.
I'm addicted to your fragrance
And your skin.
Without you, I'm a complete mess.
When I'm inside of you,
I'm at my best.
For, your love,
Body, mind and soul,
I am insatiable
Or flat out Whipped!

Luv R3

June 2, 2010 – 10:27pm

Some days, you give me,
all that you got.
On your bad days,
You give me more than,
I could ever hope for.
You are the woman,
I adore.
Your sent, your karma,
Your grace.
You put a smile on my face.
I cry tears of joy.
For, you made a man
Out of a boy.
Watching you I had to step up,
Because I wanted to marry
You my Queen.

Luv R3

June 2, 2010 – 12:41pm

What's between your thighs,
Don't keep me glued to you!
It's what your mind do.
Not the way you give me head,
or how you can roll I bed.
It's not how your weave looks,
but, how you can understand a book.
Hopefully, we shall get old,
and we are going to
Have to know each other's soul,
as Friend

Luv R3

June 3, 2010 – 5:46pm

Things I do well,
I write, speak, freak, and think,
But, I met my match.
You can say,
Ying and Yang,
And If I were a Bee,
You would be my sting,
And If you were a bird,
I'd be your wing.
We get along, like peas and carrots.
We shall feast together,
We are a mighty One.

Luv R3

June 4, 2010 – 12:32am

Have you ever needed an example?
Someone to show you the ropes,
Just like that punk',
Who showed you how to sell
And smoke dope.
Sometimes, we honor the ones,
That hurt us the most!
So, baby I respect and,
Appreciate you.
You remind me of my mother,
Who truly cares about me.
Love you baby,
Kisses.

Luv R3

June 5, 2010 – 3:57am

You're the sweetest flavor,
that comes more than once
in a chocolate supreme.
With a twist of butterscotch,
as I taste you,
my face is covered in a
sensuous cream.
So, creamy and wet,
You call out my name, as you sing.
That's when I get a second helping,
Of delicious you.
My sweet Lady,

Good to the last drop.
So, I don't stop.

                              Luv R3

June 6, 2010 – 10:46pm

Two sun and moon,
Are you and I.
Two lights that shine on the World.
Dust and Dawn,
Meeting together.
For, strength and power
to celebrate our first meeting,
SEALED WITH A KISS.
Venus has sprinkled
Magical pollen across the Heavens.
She has touched us with compassion,
Of night and day.
God woke us up,
To see us together,
Behold the power
of You and I.

                              Luv R3

June 7, 2010 – 3:05am

Three kinds of head,
That runs me.
That's in me,
that I possess in me,
I will write them,
In reverse order.

The head that's between my thighs (**OHH**)
The head that's between my ears,
Understands the head that runs
My life (**GOD**).
Baby, if you love me?
I'll give you
Plenty of head.

                              Luv R3

June 7, 2010 – 2:08pm

Time captured my every thought.
As I locked you in my heart.
In every beat of my heart,
I gave you more words,
To share our ultimate time.
My life consists of words, time, and you.
So, let us enjoy life's beautiful picture.
As I write poems to you,
And the way you made me feel.
So, now I write a painting,
A picture of love.

                              Luv R3

June 8, 2010 – 12:44am

Music of lovers strange as it may be,
It don't matter if it's Pop, Rap, or Country,
But definitely it's R&B.
Rock is even hot.
We don't stop.
Techno got moments in love,

They also sing the Blues.
But, Gospel brings' Good News'
Classical shows we are refined.
The best music is,
Our hearts beating.
We then, dance to our own drum,
So let's have fun.

                                              Luv R3

June 8, 2010 – 2:11am

When love calls your name?
Do you set quietly
Ashamed of your past?
Do shattered dreams,
Conquer your tomorrow hope?
In life there are decisions you must face.
To move forward,
to have a forefeeling life.
Choices and chances,
But the decision is yours,
To be in love or alone.
Choose wisely.

                                              Luv R3

June 9, 2010 – 1:26am

When love is profound,
It doesn't matter if it is Loud.
Yell it, in the Ghetto,
Whisper it down by the river side,
Or even on top of a mountain.

Speak it,
Believe it,
Just call it love.

Luv R3

June 9, 2010 – 3:24pm

I'm responsible to guard your heart from hurt.
For, you to breathe in serenity,
To ease your mind.
Spending every bit of my time
For you to enjoy prosperity.
And to give your mind, clarity.
So, I give you me.
Flawed, but honest and true.
On my watch, I shall protect you.
My responsibility is to change,
And guard your heart…
Even from ME!

Luv R3

June 9, 2010 – 5:10pm

There are days when I cared,
But, I didn't know how to write.
Love is patient,
Thoughtful, kind, and always
WINS.
When you do it with love.

Luv R3

June 10, 2010 – 2:51pm

It takes time to spot a jewel,
Sometimes there right in your face.
Call out your name.
Might even brush up against us,
We just have to know its value.
It maybe, cat raggedy
or shinny on one side,
but the jewel never loses,
it's valuable essence,
or its power to
Shine!

Luv R3

June 10, 2010 – 7:07pm

I just wanted you.
I didn't know who to love
I didn't know who to kiss.
Never seen grown folks holding hands,
Or even blessing there food.
How can you expect me,
The one who had a job,
When we ate at the first of the month,
And starved at the end of the month.
No stamps,
Just show our children a different way.
I just wanted you.

Luv R3

June 11, 2010 – 1:59pm

At last, I cry no more.
God gave me someone to adore.
No more feeling like a whore.
No strange relationships to ponder.
If it's right or wrong.
More than anything, I'm not alone.
'I have a mental friend
to stand with me.

Luv R3

June 12, 2010 – 12:26am

Just making love,
Is making love Saturday.
Its 12 rounds of hot, burning pain.
Naked, sweat is the only thing,
we can call clothing.
As we produce more and more,
Up and Down,
Side to Side,
A freaky ride.
Mouths open,
And eyes closed.
As we release our load to orgasm,
Round 2 we are going to
Shake up the world.

Luv R3

June 13, 2010 – 4:40am

On the first day,
of the rest of our life.
Be great, and believe,
that God has beautiful blessings
for YOU.

June 14, 2010 – 1:47am

A flower was once a seed,
But with water and sunlight,
Things just grow.
With his nurturing,
Really it's all God's Blessings.

Luv R3

June 14, 2010 – 5:51am

Many miles I travel,
Searching for my Queen,
Longing for companionship.
That understood the plight of family and friends.
In my mind,
I give up all that I could.
Until, I gave my heart,
I would have traveled a little farther,
So, I carried on,
For my true love.
A journey, worthy of its destination
Love.

Luv R3

June 14, 2010 – 9:43am

We have moments in time,
We wish that we could
get them back again.
When a grandparent,
Sibling, child, family members,
Love, or just a friend is gone or hurting badly;
Think about and cherish every moment of
togetherness.
From meals, conversation, laughter,
I Love YOU.
So, be kind.
One day it might be you.
Try a little tenderness.

Luv R3

June 15, 2010 - 3:19am

What makes us different?
Really it's just trying
and giving a piece of integrity,
morals and commitment.
See there's really no difference at all in us.
Well, OK, some of us forget one thing…
HOW TO TRY!
I think I'll try at love.
I'm half way done confessing
my love for you.
I am an all-true Man.

Luv R3

June 15, 2010-3:28pm

Who said it was going to be easy.
Who said life was not challenging?
Who thought you could call a timeout,
when life is hard?
Regardless, rich, middle class or poor,
we all deal with a situation called life.
Live up to the challenge
for it's the only life you get!
Trust in God and He shall lead you!

Luv R3

June 16, 2010 2:37am

Wisdom comes with error,
love comes from a love experience
be it yours or an elder.
Someone went through heartbreak
to get it straight.
Baby, I can say some sweet words,
but some lessons came from damaging words
that left me lonely.
So, I don't want to live that way again.
You're my best friend love.

Luv R3

June 16, 2010 10:59am

I will do my best to listen
to your stories, ideas, jokes, worries
and especially when you say I love you.

Not taking any of it for granted.
Luv R3

June 16, 2010 9:27pm

That's the time, I feel like making love...
When, I think about you,
not just seeing you,
I'm thinking about doing the do,
nasty or even screw,
grinding with you,
loving all night till noon,
admiring your moon
so sweet like a Georgia peach...
Shhh… it's time for Me. to kiss
or call me Mr. Rhodes,
if you are kind and sweet.
Luv R3

June 17, 2010 12:42pm

Why are the world's people so hard on the Black Man?
Why can't they see us as the heartbeat,
instead of a cancer?
Why do the media and other races dog us,
including our own women?
Black Men get profiled,
and are under constant scrutiny.
But, try harder and hold your head up high
my Brothers and stay strong.
May God keep you,
and HAPPY FATHER'S DAY!

United Together.

Luv R3

June 18, 2010 10:26pm

Baby, be it in a factory,
writing a book,
speaking in front of a crowd
or making a movie,
I work with a passion just like
when I'm making love to you.
Weighed, measured
and always wanting to do my best,
my testimony as a man.
I thank God for His many blessings.

Luv R3

June 19, 2010 2:46am

It's Making Love Saturday!
Faces of yesterday can't compare to your beauty,
I've been so naive.
I was a thief, stealing hearts for my own pleasure.
Kissing with lies
to get between your thighs.
What kind of man was I?
Forgive me, I was wrong.
Tell the young people in the village.
QUALITY BEATS QUANTITY,
have patience when seeking love.
Even if you're older,
have Patience.

Luv R3

June 20, 2010 1:21am Father's Day

On this Father's Day,
I have a wish.
I have all boys;
John, Jalen, Justice, Nigil, Romelo, and Randy.
Four have been with me all weekend;
but, in my heart every moment of everyday.
But, one person is missing, my little girl.
I've always wanted a baby girl.
And when my movie is finished,
I will make a "little Crystal" with my Wife,
because, "Father Am I."

Luv R3

June 21, 2010 1:40am

Traveling many miles together,
watching many moons together,
saying kind and not so kind words
towards one another,
but that's Loves Soul Food;
it was led by prayer.
Night and morning
light was started by prayer.
Relationships had good ole prayer.
You can look at some elders
and wonder why they are together;
simply, they prayed...
together.

Luv R3

June 22, 2010 1:12am

Black is beautiful, powerful, love able,
sleek, unique, commanding
with a soulful presence.
Colored from the blackest berry
to the whitest pearl
with Grey eyes.
We can't be denied
of our greatness, intelligence,
wisdom and pure brilliance;
Descendants from Kings and Queens!
Live the dream.

Luv R3

June 23, 2010 2:35am

The show must go on
regardless right or wrong,
you must move on.
Situations can be stressful.
But, you must grow
and continue the journey.
Only the strong survive.
This is a dynamic of life,
so live the best way you can!
May God bless you,
Today.

Luv R3

June 24, 2010 3:13am

Love is bold,
love keeps you warm in the cold.
Love eases the load,
love is made for the young and the old.
Love is the power in the darkest hour.
Love makes men cry
in the happiest of times,
love is blind,
love sees no color,
love is the ultimate cure
and with love we shall endure.
So, keep the faith in love.

Luv R3

June 25, 2010 10:34pm

Love is a beautiful harmony
with a sensual rhythm
that continually goes on forever.
Looking for understanding,
commitment, desire, compassion, respect
and the main ingredient,
you and me,
the Lovers.

June 26, 2010 3:14am

I am running to you,
leaving my baggage behind.
To the ladies,

I leave you this,
Lou Rawls said it best,
"You'll never find Another Love like Mine"
Now, on to better times for me,
see she is so far away,
but, I love her more every single day.
My quest is to be my best
and say I do to
YOU!

Luv R3

June 27, 2010 3:41am

What's good about something new?
For, one it's never been used,
no hang ups,
let downs
or carrying around yesterday's blues.
A fresh start is sometimes,
what's best and needed to move forward
on your journey.
Godspeed,
may peace be unto you.
Be it a career job or love
have faith, hope and
LOVE.

Luv R3

June 28, 2010 3:00am

Thank God,
He starts my day.

Then, I drive to work,
still searching for my dream.
As I drink my coffee
wondering is this the day that success
finally welcomes my blessed destiny.
So, I carry on feeling good,
because I have you.
So, I am King
because I have a Queen in you.
I work hard to share my dream with you;
my destiny's companion.
Ain't Love Grand?
It makes me a better MAN.

Luv R3

June 28, 2010 8:43pm

Just a poem for love.
There's no rules,
just I love you.
No right way,
or the perfect day,
12 months and 7 days,
that repeats.
Numbers are countless.
Time moves on,
never standing still.
Understanding God's will,
that love truly heals a broken heart,
or starts a new.
But, it will always come back

to I love you.
Never grow tired of those 3 words
Together.

Luv R3

June 29, 2010 1:51am

Just a poem.
Every new day,
We hope things will be beautiful,
We hope we make it there safely,
We hope that a special person
will be there forever with us,
We hope for meals to turn out right,
We hope that God hears our prayers,
What's life without hope?
And I hope God heard my prayer for us.
Because, what's life
without hope, faith and love?

Luv R3

*Tomorrow is the last day out of 30 and I hope she says yes!

June 30, 2010 4:23am

Alone fighting loneliness,
sitting alone on holidays,
waiting for a real love to come my way.
Going to the mall,
all I see are lovers, young and old.
It seems as if my life has been put on hold.
Alone fighting loneliness,
hoping to put this loneliness to an end.

I'm caught in a lonely shell living in a lonely hell.

Luv R3

June 30, 2010 11:35pm

No I'm not alone.
See I was taken by mental understanding;
by a woman whom I've never kissed
or embraced face to face.
I want to love mentally and spiritually
not all physically,
I want a love for eternity!
I did it with diligence
and my
WORDS.

Luv R3

*The woman is mine, true; that's one of a kind.

Rodney R. Rhodes
www.rodneyrrhodes.com
email-iwantalovethaticansee@yahoo.com

Meaning of a Father

Father am I
putting them on my shoulder,
and letting them fly?
Wiping the tears away when they cry?
Will love them until the day I die.
Working every day.
Praying God will never take them away.

Father am I
teaching them the Gospel,
and making them stand as a man?
Giving them advice to improve their lives.

Father am I?
I will punish them if they do wrong,
so a Judge won't give them a nasty home.

Father am I
telling them to do right and right shall follow?
Be a leader and trendsetter,
respecting, honoring and loving their elders.
Instilling honesty, it's the strongest force.
Can't be bent and most of all,
be a gentleman.
Use integrity at all times, and love.

Meaning of a Father

It is not a crime.

Father am I?
My dreams can be their realities.
Standing tall with their families.

Father am I
giving them a guide line?
I won't stop trying.
I Am a Father!

Rodney R. Rhodes

Soul Of A Man

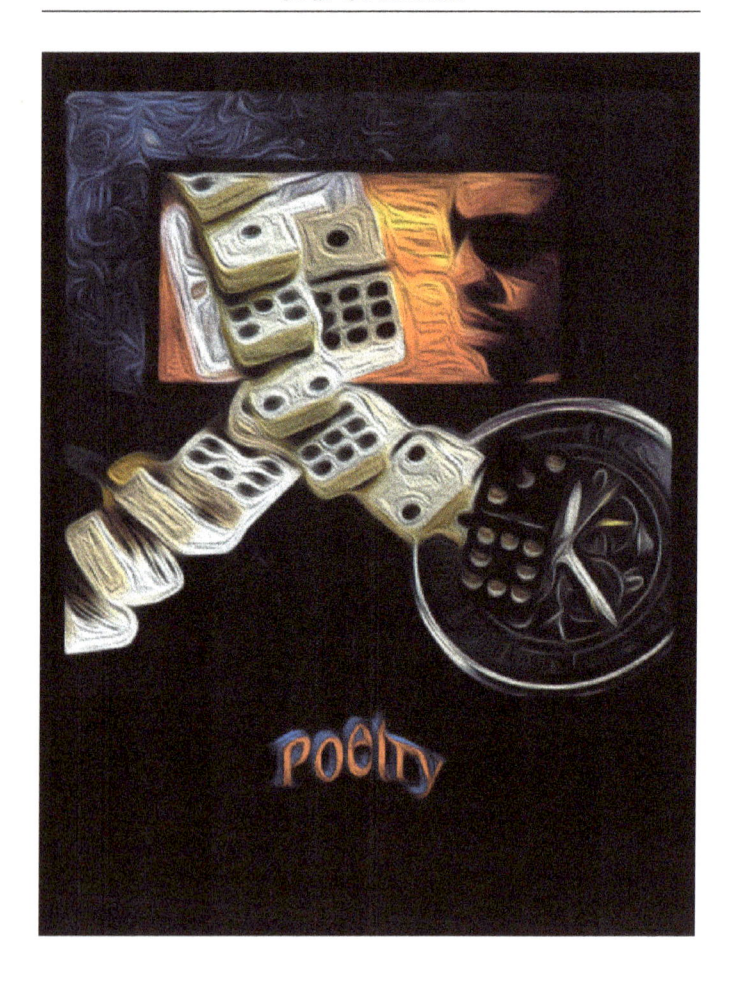

poetry

Can I sculpt U?

To the pure exotic, sensual, caring soul,
that needs to be held.
Trying to get away from their own lonely hell.
Crying out and there's no takers.

Just heart breakers, fakers, and liars.
Come go with me.
Let Ecstasy set you free.
Give me your thoughts.
Give me your mind and let me share my words.
Let me sculpt your being,
And treat you like the Queen that you are.
A Super Star.
Let's toast to you,
with your favorite glass of wine.
Let me undress your mind,
and love your soul.
Let me help you.
Feel the pleasure,
that's in your inner beauty.
Ooh wee lady, I celebrate thee.
Your sweet image, awesome karma,
and your conversation, what a revelation.
I will feed you grapes and honey dew.
I will write the most heartfelt things about you.

Let me begin sculpting,
the greatest and that is YOU!

Rodney R. Rhodes

Family Existence

No one there, but the Heavenly Father.
Sometimes friends,
and family can't see the good in me.
To ornery to quit.
To in love to move on.
To ashamed to say I'm scared.
Can't find the answer anywhere.
Falling to my knees in crowds.
Saying Help me please.
I have needs,
Though I'm not confirmed about my wants.
My family for fills my destiny.
The love of them pays me.
Children to teach.
Family to support.
My woman to love.
The village is calling my name.
It rest on my shoulders.
Captain of the ship.
Commander in chief,
to give my family existence.
Or at least to carry on,
to have a loving home.
Tears in the dark.
Smiles in the light.

Soul Of A Man

To make our world bright.
Up in the morning.
Work calling my name.
I'll put away the pain
For our family existence.

Rodney R. Rhodes

This Time I'm Going to Love Me

When you're in love.
You can't help, but kiss.
But, when the kisses become dry.
Tears will always be running wet.
Running slowly down my face.
So, I'm going to love myself
this time.
This time, I'm going to love me.
And let this beautiful bird free.
Turning again,
Searching for my best friend.
The hurt seems to understand the pain.
This time I'll be my own best friend.

Listening to my wants,
giving what I need.
Trying to let this caged bird free.
I'm lost in my soul,
And I feel the world is cold.
As a man,
I surely will be strong.
Can't let it get me down.
I need my smile,

not, an ugly frown.
God gave me his all.
So, why can't I give myself love,
And share my smile with me.
To thy own self be true.
This time, I'm going to love me,
more than I ever loved you.

May, sound vain?
Can't have stress,
When I'm trying to do my best,
Loving myself.

Rodney R. Rhodes

The Struggle

We forgot the Struggle,
The climb, the distance.
How it used to be,
now that we are free.
The world is now,
an even colder place.
Black folk still aren't equally yoked.
Trying to get by and steady buying.
Couples lying to each other.
Wanting the house on the hill,
with no love, just paying bills.
The educated laughing at the uneducated.
Uneducated with more common sense,
than the teacher with a degree.
A young man, who's an entrepreneur, goes to jail,
collects a number and a cell.
Crack and blow turning mothers into hoes,
and making fathers into nomads.
Kunta never ran from his own.
Rosa sat because she was tired, and wanted respect.
Martin dreamed because he wanted the nightmare to stop.
Madame CJ Walker comb hair because black sisters are Beautiful.
Dr. Drew made plasma to keep the blood running in our veins.
Garret Morgan makes the whole world stop.
BLACK FOLK, SO BEAUTIFUL, SO POWERFUL.

Soul Of A Man

Lift every voice and sing:
We are the real bling, bling.

Rodney R. Rhodes

A Firm ASS Whipping - No More Affirmative Action!

A firm that will not show any action,
Porters black men will be
"Shine yo' shoes boss?"

No quotas to fill.
Jobs of the past will be so unreal.
No more being a token.
They are now joking at our expense,
"Got Black?"

Ladies with attitudes, guess what?
Go hang with your girlfriends, not in our offices.
Your swagger has come to end.
May I please have a job, a loan, an education?
What's next the plantation?
This is when black folk don't stick together.
We fall to affirm with no action.
**If we don't take care of each other,
How can you expect the man
TO TAKE CARE OF A BROTHER,
SISTER, OR CHILD.**

For forty years, we did it with style.
But, not with each other.
The marches, the beatings, the tears, the love.
What were we really thinking of (self)?

400years of struggling together,
Erased in a day in Michigan.
By a firm that will not show
Any ACTION!

Rodney R. Rhodes

Hero

A young man and woman ask, "How do I become a Hero?"
Buddy Green replied
Hero's don't quit.
Hero's stand tall.
Hero's think. Hero's share.
Hero's always care.
Hero's never blame.
Hero's make hard decisions.
Hero's play for the team.
Hero's don't do it for recognition.
Heroes are willing to sacrifice.
Hero's think how to save lives.
Hero's answer the bell.
Hero's teach Hero's reach.
Hero's don't do it for fame.
Hero's do it for LOVE.
Well young people, "It's in the Soul."
Are you a Hero?

Rodney R. Rhodes

Air

Can you breathe?
If I was a cook at KFC,
Could I cook you dinner?
If I was the Garbage Man,
Would you let me kiss your hand?
If I was the local Auto Plant Worker,
Would you let me rub you down with hot oils?
If I was the Lawn Man,
Would you let me bring you flowers?
If I was the Plumber,
Could I run your bath?
If I was an unknown writer,
Could I write you poetry?
Well, I'll speak for a lot of African American Men,
And I'll say if I could be your air,
I'll let you breath.
Do you want to **EXHALE**?

Rodney R. Rhodes

My Big Brother Could Rap

I LOVE you.
Thanks to rhythm and blues.
You gave me words of tenderness,
to understand her mind, soul, and body.
Made it a private party.
Gave me heart,
And words of David Ruffin, Otis Redding,
Luther Vandross and Ron Isley.
Smokey Robinson chased the tears away.
Marvin Gaye made it a beautiful day.
Harold Melvin and the Blue notes
sent me a Teddy bear name Mr. Pendergrass,
To give it to you.
So, you could hear my Whispers,
due to the sweet sounds of the Spinners.
Just growing like the
Temptations that I had for you.
Stevie Wonder told me,
That I didn't need light, to hold you tight.
Barry White said just the way you are.
Sam Cooke knew that you would send me.
Frankie Lyman shouted why fools fall in love.
Freddie Jackson knew to take it nice and slow.
Bill Whithers said use me till you use me up.
And then the O'jays interrupted and sang loving you.

Soul Of A Man

So, it didn't have to be hard
to say I want you for my very own.
Then my heart played another slow jam.
And the Jackson gave me five,
and Prince made me a King.
Here and Now,
Thanks Big Brothers.
Now, I can share my thoughts
with a LADY.

Rodney R. Rhodes

Every Time the Wind blows think of Him

I was walking, and crying.
Wishing things could be better.
Then a mighty wind came.
My eyes closed, and I was taken on a journey.
The wind touched me.
It surrounded my body.
It caressed me from head to toe.
It whispered in my ear.
It held me like no other lover.
It blew me in directions,
that I couldn't even fathom.
It was the first time something had my back.
And it wouldn't let go.

It wiped my tears away,
with one gentle breeze.
It even knocked me down to my knees.
Had me praying to God Almighty.
Then the wind started to sing,
You are my child.
And I am YOUR FATHER.
When the wind stop blowing,
My life had a new meaning.

Soul Of A Man

The turbulence shook my hope,
and renewed my faith.
God blew his love into me,
Forever more.
I shall get down on my knees and pray.
God Whispered,
I am here every day.
Talk to ME.

Rodney R. Rhodes

All Along

That finger print on the Landmark building on campus,
opened my eyes from darkness.
I took the campus for granted.
I laughed at the chipped paint on the walls.
Never thinking about the man,
who gave his life for that wall to stand tall.
I giggled at the admissions building,
when the bricks fell down.
Never thinking about the woman,
who paid giving up her Life.
I cursed when the lights went off in the dorm.
Never thinking about the students,
who had read by candlelight.
Somehow, I never thought about Our past.
Until, I saw that finger print on the Landmark building.
I knew then, they were thinking about me,
all along.

Rodney R. Rhodes

Cupid's Arrow

Acquaintance not knowing the description of his valor.
Until, Cupid's arrow scissor through her beautiful flesh.
Now, she's wanting his heart and needing his soul,
to entwine the feelings that matches her integrity.
To create an empire full of love and understanding,
So they build and beautify thy world.
Cupid's arrow maneuvers through all walks of life.
Love is taking flight and brings a consciousness
to jesters, kings, and fools alike.
Independence is not needed,
Wealth is in honor,
Not in financial gain.
As the stars are visible for all to see.
Cupid's arrow keeps attacking her and me.
It is making a loving family.

Rodney R. Rhodes

Who's next in line, your son or mine?

I was listening to hard core Rap.
They were talking about popping MF Moet tops.
I thought about the children, who didn't have anything to eat,
using profanity like it was all they were taught.

I was listening to hard core Rap.
They were talking about screwing two Ghetto &8#@! I
thought about the man and woman who had STD's.

I was listening to hard core Rap.
They were talking about Spinners and Daytons.
I thought about brothers in wheel chairs, hit
from stray bullets during a drive by.

I was listening to hard core Rap.
They were talking about making M-O-N-E-Y.
I thought about all the young men,
who had dreams of riches, and fame.
Slanging those things,
to end up on a modern day plantation,
broke and in captivity.

I was listening to hard core Rap.

Soul Of A Man

They were talking about babies mama's drama.
I thought about the fatherless children,
who had no one to call daddy.

I was listening to hard core Rap.
They were talking about the good life, and having respect.
I thought about how many drug dependent people,
we're stilling to get high.
Women selling their bodies to get a buzz.
How many children were dropping out of school?
They are trying to be next in line to be known as the Man.
I thought about how many more brothers would go to jail.
How many black women searching for a man,
lowering their standards.
Acting like a video queen,
walking half naked, trying to get attention.
How many more brothers buried six feet deep?
RAP-PED in silk suits, and with gold around their necks,
and a hint of bling, bling.

Now, that is the Hard Core Truth.
Holler, if you hear me.
Due to being hard,
Listening to lies on the Radio.
How to be a Ruff Neck, a Pimp, a Hustler, a Baller,
Bout it, Bout it, Niggas.
We are losing every day.

How can it change,
If our kids can only see,

and hear gloom and doom.

Rodney R. Rhodes

Out of This World

The dreams of the unknown pure,
To the universe clouded,
To the soul, it's pure as gold.
Serenity breaking the galaxy down.
Taking the Milky Way for a journey.
Venus weeping for understanding.

Mars crying for love.
Comets flying with no destination.
Pluto being so far,
but needing to be touched.
Crying for togetherness,
millions of miles away from sunlit skies.

Fire flies lighting up country skies.
The beauty of a heavenly angel.
In darkness she's my northern star.
Leading me home to wish upon.
And you are that STAR.
Shine, shine, and release the feelings,
that I yearn for.
Now, light the way to love.

Rodney R. Rhodes

Priceless

One moment is all it took.
Glance of infatuation.
Pure communication.
Words of endearment made for lady.
Spoken by gent.
Sweetie, honey, sweet baby,
One foxy lady and of course love.
In the rhapsody of two.
I and you entwined by the mind.
Blossoming and doing fine.
Up right, and holding on.
Structure of the Eiffel Tower.
Making love in the mist of the rain.
You are my spectrum.
My Super bowl, my get high, my cognac,
my dance, my Ace of Spade, my every pleasure.
How do I measure your worth?
PRICELESS.

Rodney R. Rhodes

1 + 1

Mountains to climb.
Lakes to swim.
Fields to run through.
Sun sets to gaze into.
Peaches to taste.
Without you it's a waste.

Stars to wish upon.
Skinny dip in a pond.
Roses to share.
Kisses to tell us,
we care.
Without you none of this exist.

Ooh wee,
The formula for LOVE.
No hang ups.
Just us smiling.
No friends telling us,
How and why.
This love is about, you and I.
I don't want to waste a minute,
On not loving you.

1+1

Let's share the world and always stay true.
(My heart on Love)

Rodney R. Rhodes

A True Poem (in the making of Randy)

Once upon a time there was a fool called me.
I thought I was special to the ladies.
I always gave and never asked for a dime.
I could leave at any time.
See my mission was to never fall in love.
I was a player what!
Light ones, tall ones, darks ones too,
but my heart was so untrue.
Lonely nights were far and between,
cause I freaked many queens.
Never saying you are my lady,
running away from commitment.
Like an outlaw running from a posse.
Then out of nowhere, I fell deep in love.
And it knocked me off my feet.
Now, I'm reaping all those tears that I have caused.
All the emotions, the wondering, and the mighty why.
Guess what?
Even players cry.
That fool was me.
I'm praying God, please hear my plea!

A True Poem (in the making of Randy)

Bring my true love back to me,
Forgive me.

Rodney R. Rhodes

Deeper than a Video

The Beauty of a woman cannot be compared.
She is the morning air.
She is the flower that lives in all seasons.
She's the only reason men chase gold.
Without her there's no goal.
She's the prized possession.
She's worth every sacrifice.
She gives life to thy world.
She's the Mother pearl.
She makes the cold days hot,
and hot days burning with passion.
She is the fruit in the wine.
She comes across my mind
a million times.
Her essence is heaven sent.
She makes the baddest man a gent.
Her touch, her glow,
she's the perfect star.
I pray and wish for that
Beautiful Woman.

Rodney R. Rhodes

From a Dream to a NIGHTMARE

The Black man's fall from glory,
The village called it a horror story.
Once upon a time a King,
now a jester.
Life has turned into a disaster.
Enslavement, now called a jail cell.
Now his woman wishes him hell.
No jobs, no licenses, no permits,
and in fear he quits.

Picking up a gun or drug to ease the pain.
He's slowly going insane.
Children with his eyes.
Now despise the very sight of him.
Life has become grim.
CBS, ABC, NBC, and CNN,
MAKE SURE THE PAINTING IS DARK AND UGLY.
The image of a killer, and a thief.
The whole world sees me as the cancer,
and there is no cure.

Incapable of being trusted, or loving.
3/5 of a man, it still stands.

Soul Of A Man

A drug dealer, a car stealer, getting high,
Don't care if I live or die.
If I'm neat and clean,
My sister wants to know which way I swing.
Am I on the down low?
And you ask me how low a brother can
go, when everyone else got us
living in hell on earth.
Nobody, but nobody believes in me.
That is my society.
I guess God will have to watch over me.
My taxes are higher than my car.
Inner city schools have more cutbacks,
than any town in the state.
But, we play the lottery like it is a religion.
Praying for a hit.
My gas and my lights cost more than my rent.

No help from my state.
My kids can't even celebrate a birthday.
I rob Peter to pay Paul.
And I, the black man take the fall.
The black man is still not free.
The head of my house,
Now weak as a mouse.

When I stand up and fight,
The law makers say:
Good night (Malcolm, Huey, Shaka, Nat,
Medgar, and Martin).

From a Dream to a NIGHTMARE

The horror story, Black folk it's time for a new story.

>Let's bring the dream back from 1968.
>It's time for the sleeping Giant to wake!

>>*Rodney R. Rhodes*

Black Folk – Calling 911

It's an emergency, save us!
Our babies,
so tender in black shade.
Descendants of former slaves,
Our Ancestors were Kings and Queens with huge dreams.
They have so far to go.
Teach them love.
Reach their hearts.
Build their minds.
Crave integrity and speak of honesty.
If we don't teach them it is a travesty.
Stand up and do the right thing.
Women, teach our girls to be ladies.
Men, stop letting prison be your home.
Women can't do it alone.
Old men, inspire our boys to do right.
Reverends, preach from the soul,
and reach outside the church doors.
To the community:
People, give our children heroes.
Entertainers, find another subject.
Pimps, hoes, guns, and drugs
Have killed a generation.
Our children deserve better.
Educate their minds,

Black Folk – Calling 911

And leave a legacy of brilliance.
Teachers it's more than a job.
Our children will make us proud.
Build our children's minds, and
save our world, country, state,
City, family, home, us, you,
Me and our children.

Rodney R. Rhodes

Just Keep Coming!

Crying for a man is unbecoming,
When it comes to love.
Taught to be rugged and hard.
See emotions don't live here,
When she's not around.
I steer weakness and I rebuke stress.
But, without her,
I'm never my best.
Her love brings me to my knees.
In winter, she's my spring breeze.
She's my light in dark times.
She's my writing.
She's the love that's on my mind.
With her unity and faithfulness goes hand in hand.
And I'm more of a Man.
I stand in bliss,
The warmth of her kiss.
Her laughter is my song.
I'll play it over and over again.
She's my best friend.
Yes, I cry tears of joy.
I know its love.
And I'll keep coming toward her,
For she's the one I'm dreaming of.
For she is honor, my realm, my light.

Just Keep Coming!

The true essence of my life.
Captivating, spiritual, relating is she becoming
my existence of all that is true.
Overwhelmed by the mere sight of you.
So, I close my eyes and pray.
But, first I thank God for you.
For letting my dreams become true.
How deep in love I am with you,
How Becoming.

Rodney R. Rhodes

Miracle Worker

I'm growing and I feel new.
I'm leaving the wrongs behind,
I won't let them corrupt my mind.
I feel strong this time.
I belong.
Won't let you intimidate my soul.
Jesus has a hold on my roots.
My feet are planted in His spirit.
I'm reaching for His grace.
He wiped the tears from my face.
He touched my heart.
I'm precious ART.
I was designed by Jesus.
I was made to last,
and withstand man's abuse.
To honor my faith in Him.
He's my Rock, my Sword, and my Shield.
I will do God's will.
He has healed me.
My Miracle Worker,
Who doesn't take Holidays or Breaks.
Because He knows I'll make a mistake,
because He knows I'm just a man.

Miracle Worker

And He'll have to heal me
Once Again.

Rodney R. Rhodes

Bridging the Gap

A voice of a child said help me!
Reach back,
My soul needs your strength.
My mind needs your patience.
My heart needs your love.
Our people need me,
to carry on our legacy.
Every waking minute,
and every hour we need solutions.
We need to bridge this gap.
We need to close all that is apart.
So, we can bring an ill society to good health again.
We must become partners and friends.
We all need to shoulder our plight.
Put morals back into our life.
The bridge is still in demand.
Every woman and every man,
even children too.
Put them together,
And that's humanitarian glue.
We need every one of you,
Speaking out when something is wrong.
Being a trendsetter,
Being strong,
Put love into our community.

Bridging the Gap

Build from within, and
educate a young mind.
Never stop trying to bridge the gap.
Put spirit back into our elders.
They have carried us long enough.
Give us hope.
Give us pride.
When you left out the door,
You sang, "That's What Friends Are For."
We need you even more.
We need family.
We need to bridge the gap.
And believe that we won't be apart anymore.
If we start with understanding, From one side to another.
Finally, we can be called brothers and sisters.
If only we can bridge the gap with
Love.

Rodney R. Rhodes

Taste Great and less Feelings

It's just not true.
I thought so highly of you.
My world was turning for the better.
I loved you with every letter.
I counted my blessings,
Every time I laid my eyes on you.
Birds sang a lovely melody.
Flowers bloomed, and the man on the moon smiled.
Grass had sarsaparilla entwined,
and you were my sweet sensation.
Tastier than cotton candy.
It's not true.
How could you become bitter?
It's not true.
My sweet love left, with a bitter soul.
And now, I have a sad face.
And I cry:
Sometimes love loses its taste.

Rodney R. Rhodes

You Better Date Calvin
(Mickey D's Guy)

Young girl,
Why are you bringing shit into your world?
Looking for that baller,
With his diamond bracelet and gator boots.
He's totting a 357, sending folks to heaven.
He's using the words fu---k and bit--h.
He's living a death wish,
Selling the devil's drug.
Young girl can you find a real man to hug?
You better date Calvin.

Calvin got longevity.
He'll be educated in 4 to 5 years.
Why big baler calling you from the state pen?
Now, you're his only friend.
The streets have forgotten him,
or poured a little liquor on his behalf.
Leaving babies from the west to the east side.
You only liked him for his ride.
Big rims, his hairdo, and Money,
For a little of your honey.

Soul Of A Man

Now, Calvin driving and living large.
The geek was always the strong one.
Not the one,
who had to walk with the crowd.
But, the one who made his own path.
Riding the bus, getting up early to make it to class.
And being your baller's lawyer,
Trying to save his ass.
You better date Calvin.

Rodney R. Rhodes

My Greatest Dance Partner

Our dance, our footsteps, our rhythm,
The way we move together.
The balance and the grace.
The magic that comes over us,
when we embrace.
Holding hands, as man and woman.
Understanding and planning to be one.
Our day has come.
Today, we unite as love.
No matter the place,
no matter the music,
we shall dance as Husband and Wife.
My greatest dance partner in life.
Our journey begins with a million steps,
with my best friend.
Gliding through a timeless dance.
A forever waltz,
the immortal tango.
We swing, we dance with love.

Rodney R. Rhodes

Destiny

Tell me your fantasy.
But, remember you are my destiny.
All other lovers stop.
I'm at the center of your heart.
You are the only name wrote on mine.
It began with our first kiss.
Since, I was a child,
You've been at the top of my wish list.
No toy, nor game,
You are all I wish for.
Even now, I love you more and more.
The birds sing.
The leaves stay green.
The sun continues to shine,
and you are forever mine.
My power, my plight, my love,
my destiny.

Rodney R. Rhodes

Your Company I don't Need!

Misery loves thy company.
It has thorns to warm thy blood.
Heartache to control thy mind.
Darkness to cover thy eyes.
Revenge to submerge thy good spirit.
Hate to tame thy love.
Misery puts the ugly into a beautiful world.
Greed out of a giving life.
Misery is company,
that I do not need.
I say leave me alone.
I shall smile with me.
And cast the miserable to the side.
My life has a goal,
not to be miserable.

Rodney R. Rhodes

I'd Rather Walk in my HOOD

Ride the bus and catch me at the Diner,
Where I can sit in front of you,
or Side by Side.
Looking eye to eye asking:
"Why did you hurt us so back then?
And now we still cry.
We have the blues.
Too much bad news.
Two million black men on lock down.
Still slavery exists.
Creating a future where grown men kiss.
Little boys dying before 25,
through prison or violence.
Little ladies trying to find Mr. Right,
Slim pickings.
Jobs and businesses in our community have decayed.
Reverends preaching and not reaching.
In the schools, we are educating fools.
Who don't believe,
Prayer got us through the boycotts.
The knight rider and strange fruit which was us,
that HUNG from a tree.
Now, material goods have us reaching,

I'd Rather Walk in my HOOD

for importance of money, cars, diamonds and gold.
But, this is not the goal.
I'm at the bus. Stop!
Waiting for the next march;
Waiting for the next march;
Listening for Sam Cook to sing a Change Gonna Come.
Martin to say, I HAVE A DREAM,
and MALCOLM by any means necessary.
But, all I hear is I'm a hustler, pimp, and a player.
That said, "Revolution won't be Televised" Look
at our community, destroyed day by day.
As, I ride to your community to work, cook, and clean.

Rodney R. Rhodes

Flower

Promises and laughter.
Fools like riddles with no answers.
Lights in the sky,
in day time and night too.
My light was you.
I found my heart in your soul.
I felt warmth, when it was cold.
We were wrapped in each other's embrace.
Every morning, I was awakened to your beautiful face.
A flower that only needed love to grow.
So, you grew.
Because, I could only think of you.
Love is all I have.
So, I feed you love.
I watched you Blossom.
I smiled.
I cried tears of joy, and watered
you with my happy tears.
I release your fears,
And kiss the petals.
To let you know,
our love will always
grow.

Rodney R. Rhodes

Passion for Lust

Her beauty was in my sight.
My plight on loving tonight.
Dreams of passion are a constant fight.
I lose myself in my own mind.
Every love story has a villain and his name is me.
With no shame nor cause,
To stampede a damsel's mind and body.
With my laws of righteousness and purity,
caught between good and lust.
Removing one leg at a time at bed side.
What comes over my mind,
is the beauty of her explicit hips.
I lose myself in sexual bliss.
That starts with a kiss.
Not knowing why,
I chase the Queen.
But, I must satisfy my animal being.
A fantasy takes over me, so scared of giving that one heart.
My very own,
but deep down I'm so all alone.
I want her more and more.
Now, I can share my thoughts with
A Lady.

Rodney R. Rhodes

Blame Me

Streets lights come on,
and kids are still in the streets.
Drugs on the table,
With no danger label.
Gun with no hunters, just killers.
Sex with no protection, just an erection.
A Marvin Gaye song,
but with b*$@h and whoe;
instead of Baby or Love.
What's going on?

Twisted values.
How educated we have become.
But, why are we so dumb?
Integrity and Morals are now nasty.
We have lost our roles in life.
Now, women want a wife.
Men have become dog's best friend, locked in a cage.
Why do we behave inhumane?
Have we made life into a game?
Stress has concurred our brain.
To say, I don't give a damn,
get in where you fit in,
is a sin.

Blame Me

Slowly losing my religion.
No more marching against the white man.
I think it's time to blame me,
The BLACK Man.
For my choices,
I've let many people down,
Who gave up their LIFE for my freedom!
What's going on?
I'll take the blame!
We must first, look at ourselves
as the leader of our homes.
Again, blame me,
I was Wrong.

Rodney R. Rhodes

Sabotage

Sabotage amongst the ranks.
Can we really put all the blame on the white man?
Planes come in bringing cocaine.
Does that mean we should
sell it to our community and friends.
Churches on every corner.
Why do little black kids still hunger?
Teachers with all the knowledge, can't
get black kids in college.
At one time, we could only be share croppers.
Now, we can't even think about owning a grocery store,
with fresh vegetables.
In 1955 Rosa wanted to sit at the front of the bus.
Now, our kids rush to the back.
We keep sliding.
The most unity we have is in the Chicago step,
and the Hustle.
Sabotage in the ranks.

We use to care about what our neighbors would think.
Now, we don't care about our families as much.
We scream out I can do it on my own.
Black women raising families on their own.
Money can only buy a house.
Without love it won't be a home

Sabotage

You'll still be alone.

More brothers in jail in the USA,

Than people living in Cleveland and Detroit together.

Now, that's slavery.

Now, tell me how many kids are growing up without fathers?

You do the math.

I'll tell you it's time to clean our house.

Too much SABOTAGE.

Damn, too much SABOTAGE in the ranks.

Rodney R. Rhodes

Me, Myself, and I. What a Lie!

Doing it as I see fit,
But some things not fitting.
Life got rough.
I'm thinking bad luck got my number.
Troubled winds blowing.
Good things were happening,
Few and far between.
My heart started to get mean.
My dreams started to become nightmares.
What happened to the person that used to care?
With a smile, I thought God's love would always be there.
And more losing came my way.
Walking, asking, "Why oh why, is it happening to me?
What have I done to deserve this?
Too much to bare.
I tried to run.
I ran as fast as, my legs would carry me. But,
I got tired and I fell to my knees.
I finally called Jesus on my knees.
I looked into my soul and said,
I can't walk it alone.
I did all I could do.
Jesus, I need you.

Me, Myself, and I. What a Lie!

I raised my arms high.
Tears, I started to cry.
I was humbled.
Thinking it was all about me.
When Jesus was carrying me.
I jumped from His loving arms,
And started to dance.
Saying me, myself, and I.
Soon after that, I started to cry.
I was living a lie.
Without his grace, I'm nothing.
Nothing shall prosper.
I need you dear, Lord.
Things started to change.
I felt I wasn't the same.
I was better.
I called on him and he answered.
I shall never leave YOU.
But, it is what you choose to do.
Jesus is back on the Throne,
Head of my life.

Rodney R. Rhodes

*To Rodney R. Rhodes
from Donald Goines:
You Better Man Up!*

The vibe of a pimp, and a player,
Drugs, and the undertaker,
Money and good booze.
Brothers only making the action news.
On a deal gone bad,
stories of death and deceit.
Tags on the toes of young feet.
Lies, and tears, and drive-byes.
Ghetto women looking for a way out,
Calling for ballers with street clout.
I'll pawn anything for blow?
Got ass to sell or show!
My self-esteem is at zero.
I'm calling from the depths of despair.
Can't find anybody to care.
Another brother man going nowhere.
Visions of abandoned buildings,
and CRACK addicts.
Once, and a while seeing someone dead.
From black on black crime.

When I'm only fourteen,
Why should I try?
I'm too young for my dreams
To die.

Rodney R. Rhodes

Difference in US

The sun that shines on the wealthy,
Shines on the poor.
A friend will always let you in their door.
A loving person will feed the poor.
A child will cry for kindness.
A man that's blind will ask for light.
A thief will ask for love.
A liar will ask for honesty.
Someone with no pride,
Will ask for integrity.
One, who believes,
Will ask why the innocent die.
The ones who use drugs,
Don't want pain.
The gifted are going insane.
People who fly,
Want to ride the train.
Framers wish for rain.
Mothers wish for companionship,
Fathers look for lovers.
Children want parents at 30,
To redeem what was lost from 5 to 18.
Why is the world so mean?
I dream.
I believe.

Difference in US

Where did the hurt come from?
I just want someone to take my advice.
It's hard living life.
I just want to be right.
Listen to me,
I'm yelling and nobody hears me.
Stop fighting, stealing,, killing, and cheating.
Give me life.
Do right.
Smile with me tonight.
The pleasure is to know you, my neighbor.
Love me as I love you.
Let's love, when the bombs fall.
Who would you yearn for
Your child, your parent, your mate, your GOD,
or even money?
Knowing it won't mean a Damn.
Chasing it for so long.
You forgot that the whales are gone,
Like the dinosaurs, and polar bears too.
Next?
I and You.

Rodney R. Rhodes

In the Blink of an Eye

In the blink of an eye,
tears of the lonely cry.
Hand never being held in,
many moons and many tales.
Thoughts of happiness; bewitched by a lover's spell.
Temptation longing to capture a soul,
But, in the morning no one near to hold.
Thieves taken love at random,
giving nothing in return.
But, sometimes the strong must learn how to be weak,
when love knocks them off their feet.
One question comes to mind.
Why was it me?
The strongest of thee.

Rodney R. Rhodes

Today

Today is a new day, so full of promise.
Dreams of a fruitful life welcome your embrace.
Thoughts of joy and bliss will overwhelm yesterday's misuses.
So, savor the essence of your existence.
Thank God for your blessings and short comings.
His power will carry your burdens, ease your pain,
And let love share your new day.

Rodney R. Rhodes

Hired Help

Walking without a clue.
Needing you,
and bumping my head.
Constantly, learning on the run.
Can't find the right advice,
for life and it's challenges.
Male teachers are gone by three.
Now, it's just me.
No authority to say good job,
Or even you are wrong.
But, my muscles are strong.
Here alone with my brute strength,
to solve my many problems.
When an apology would have been the solution.
Daddy where are you?
A question of a fatherless child searching,
and wondering how to be a Man?
Really, I don't have a plan.
Learning on the job of life,
and I hopefully I won't be terminated.
I'm worthy of this position called
MAN!

Rodney R. Rhodes

Numbers

Poem about numbers.
You give **BILLIONS** of dollars for a war in Iraq,
after losing 5000 people on 9/11.
Well, count how many blacks we lost in
the U.S. of A on our soil,
year by year because of black on black crime in Detroit,
St Louis, Los Angeles, Chicago District of
Columbia, Miami, Memphis, Philadelphia,
Houston, Cleveland, Atlanta, and New York.
Then count the smaller cities in between.
Ask how many people called 911 tax payers,
who lost children for the lack of
Family education and jobs.
But, you built
up another country while we at fighting in our own country.
We are at battle in our own country building jails,
or slave quarters to lock up young minds away forever.

Here's a math problem for a U.S. of A;
Count those 12 cities, times it by 250 murders, and then add 200
representing every killer caught, times it by 12,
then add it up and then times that by ten (for ten years),
next times that by 2.5 for every child left behind,
add it up all together, well if you believe

in 6 degrees of separation,
I knew all of them.
Speaking for my family; it hurts Oh darn!
I forgot all the cities in between the 12.
Back to the drawing board,
math is really hard, but writing I can handle.

Rodney R. Rhodes

The Wise Man On The Corner Series

Family

Family

One hot day on the city's east side, near the corner of 5th and Sexton, a troubled young man by the name of Mark Culbreth; just happened to cross the path of a wise older man named Buddy Green. Buddy Green was sitting on a crate right outside of Prince Bern's Wine Store. "Tell me, old timer, why can't we just walk away from these tired women?"

"Well, you can young man, but you're going into another, then another. And next thing you'll know, you'll be tired too. So, love the one you're with, and maybe she will love your tired butt." He laughs. Mark said, "But, you're right though; they're all basically the same. Every day after work when I get home I'm hit with a barrage of do- this and don't-do that stuff. "Why don't you spend time with the kids, the grass needs cutting, don't smoke in the house, you know, you drink entirely too much beer, yada, yada, yada." Damn! I might as well have stayed at work where at least I'd get paid to get harassed."

"Yeah, yeah young man. She sounds like a real pest, but if you think about it, it could be worse. When I was your age, the exact same thing happened to me. And I felt just like you, like I was being pestered, but let me tell you, you'll miss the hell out of it when you don't have it anymore. I know. My wife and kids up and left and man let me tell you, the so-called nagging isn't nearly as bad as coming home to an empty house. Your woman staying on you; just shows that she loves and cares for you. I remember once an old man told me a story about1/4 Wait a minute, do I have time to tell you about it, yeah, yeah. I've got time. Here young fella. Take this extra crate and take a load off and let me tell you this story about our people and what we've been going through. You'll see then that your problem is nothing to get bent out of shape about."

Buddy Green tells the story of a slave named **MUSTAFA**.

Mustafa was a young king in Africa. One day while taking a stroll through the bush; all of a sudden several men jumped him. He had been captured by slave traders. They shackled him; put him on a ship with several hundred more slaves; and shipped them across the great ocean America. After what seemed to be an eternity at sea; the ship finally arrived in Virginia and him along with all the others who survived the journey, were auctioned off to the highest bidders. Mustafa had never felt more humiliated. They checked his teeth, the crack of his butt, his hands, feet and the fact he had a physique like chiseled bronze. The auctioneer yelled at Mustafa, "Turn your big black ass around nigger, "but Mustafa didn't understand. The auctioneer then struck him with a thick whip. The immediate excruciating pain caused Mustafa to wince and with the second strike of the whip, Mustafa grabbed it and snatched it out of the auctioneer's hand. Mustafa quickly returned the favor; right upside the head. The auctioneer fell down in complete agony. Every white person within

Family

range made a mad dash to get out of the way. Mustafa was now cracking the whip at nearly anyone who got close. The auctioneer, who had now gotten up and out of the way, ran over to his horse and reached into his saddle bag. His hand emerged from the saddlebag with a revolver. He began to make his way back over towards Mustafa. As the auctioneer slowly raised the pistol towards Mustafa, all of a sudden Mustafa dropped to the ground in a heap. A beautiful little black woman was standing over him with a piece of wood in her hand. She unknowingly, had just saved Mustafa's life. Mustafa was chained to a tree and whipped unmercifully; stopping just short of killing him.

Mustafa and the pretty little black woman were both sold to Jake Johnston, one of the big land owners in the area for $30. The auctioneer probably would have gotten more for Mustafa, but he had been left nearly dead. Ironically, 20 years later, Mustafa has three children now; with the beautiful little black woman, who had saved his life years earlier. Her name is Candice. She is a beautiful caramel colored little woman with green eyes. And she sang like an angel. There was another daughter by the name of Star, whose father was Master Jake. Mustafa loved Star like she was his very own, although he knew that she wasn't. Even though Mustafa had now been in this land more than 20 years now, he still yearned to walk through the bush freely; back in his native land. Realistically, he could only wonder. His family was his world. His kids were his pride and joy. Candice was his strength. That vigor that his family gave him made him a tireless worker. He'd be ready to plow when the mule was ready to quit was the local saying. And believe you me, Master Jake knew for a fact that he had made quite the steal when he purchased Mustafa, but he hadn't dreamed Mustafa was going to be this good. For that reason, Master Jake made sure that is foreman kept a keen eye on Mustafa, still after all these years, afraid Mustafa would run away.

"I've got to check on my fruit" referring to Candice and any of his other slave women; who at his urges he would just "take" when he felt like it. This is probably the reason Mustafa worked so hard. Beat the mule harder than the master beat any of his slaves; will help take the pain away was his thinking. Only at sunset; would Mustafa and his family be allowed to actually 'come together' as a whole. But even then, there was no guarantee that the family wouldn't all of a sudden get rudely interrupted by the urges of Master Jake. What must have seemed like every night to Mustafa; Master Jake would come to the house a couple times a week, usually drunk, and always there for Candice. There have been several occasions where Mustafa just wanted to go outside and put a stop to this nonsense. One night in particular, a drunken Master Jake showed up looking for Candice. He's standing outside and yells for her to come out. Mustafa had enough. Candice tried to stop him, but to no avail.

"Leave my wife be" he yelled at Master Jake. "Boy, get back in the house and send Candice out," retorted Master Jake. "I own both your asses, and I'll do as I please with my property." One day Master Jake got some

Family

really bad news. He owed quite a bit of money to lenders. He would have to sell some of his property; to pay his ever-growing bills. He called for a meeting of all slaves and foreman. The meeting was held up at the big house, outside of course. Once everyone had assembled Master Jake stepped out. I'm afraid I have some bad news. I have to sell a lot of my property. As of tomorrow, a lot of you will no longer be here, foreman included. Everyone left the meeting shaking their heads. The foremen could go find new employment; but too the slaves that meant that a great deal of them would be soul; and not necessarily to the same place. They were scared.

Mustafa was no exception. After working in the fields that day, Mustafa and his family got together for dinner. After dinner, everyone got ready for bed. All of a sudden, Master Jake showed up outside yelling for Candice. Mustafa hopped out of bed, mad as a wet hornet. Candice tried in vain again to stop him. "Leave my wife be, you hear", yelled Mustafa. No sooner than he'd gotten those words out his mouth a whip cracked in the air. Mustafa was knocked to the ground. A couple of Master Jake's foremen whipped Mustafa until he passed out from pain. Master Jake then went in to see Candice to satisfy his urges. When he'd finished and had left, Candice gathered herself and went outside to gather her husband. He was a complete mess. They had beaten him badly and had poured liquor on his wounds. She nursed his many open wounds as best she could. He kissed Candice, rubbed the kid's heads and slowly walked out the door. He crawled into the wagon and off they went.

They rode for a couple of hours, before they finally came to stop at this big field by a lake. Mustafa had never been to this place before. But, as usual it didn't matter. He started plowing. In the meantime, Master Jake and one of his foremen left. They didn't get back; until much later that day. Mustafa crawled into the wagon and off they went for home. They dropped Mustafa off at his doorstep. He went inside. It was very quiet. He called for Candice, but there was no reply. The kids weren't around either. Mustafa ran back outside. Master Jake was still there.

"I sold the whore and the little monkeys", he replied. Mustafa dropped to his knees and cried out. Master Jake left him right there. The next morning, the foreman came to pick up Mustafa. Mustafa came out and crawled into the wagon. He hadn't slept a wink last night. He lay in the back of the wagon and sang. When they'd gotten back to the field again Master Jake is already there. "Sleep alright last night boy" he said to Mustafa. Mustafa didn't answer.

He went right to plowing. After a couple rows, he stopped. "Get back to work boy" the foreman yelled. Mustafa walked over to the edge of the lake, he looked into the sky started singing again and jumped into the lake. Master Jake yelled to the foreman to go fetch Mustafa. The foreman replied, "I can't swim!"

Master Jake jumped into the lake. He got hold of Mustafa, but not only was Mustafa much stronger, his will was strong, and he wanted to die. He grabbed Master Jake, and down they both went to their watery grave.

Family

"That's a very sad story" Mark exclaimed. He said, "But, I don't get it. Why did Mustafa just kill himself?" Now, if that was me, I would have tried to find my family." "Just a minute", said Buddy Green. He said, "Back in those days, you couldn't just leave the plantation or go search. You would have had to run away. That could and a lot of times did get slaves killed; if they got caught. The best thing to have done would have been to escape to the North. Besides, you didn't know if your family had been sold as a whole unit, or if they were split up. On top of that, you wouldn't have had a clue, as to where to begin your search." "I would have tried", said Mark. "That's exactly the point; I' m trying to make young man. No sacrifice is too much for the sake of family, so let me be the one to tell you. "Make a serious effort to become your woman's best friend, no matter the cost. Because, once they're gone; they're not coming back. Take it from an old fool. "I'd like to thank you kindly for that bit of advice", said Mark. "I have to go home now and work on that very same thing. God Bless you." Mark walked away with a renewed pep in his step. As for Buddy Green; he can still be found sitting on a crate outside, and giving out bits of advice.

Drugs

Drugs

It's just another typical day at the corner of 5th and Sexton. Bullets rang out in rapid session, people scattering in all directions attempting to escape another senseless onslaught. Yet, on his curbside crate Buddy Green sits perched, barely flinching at the latest episode of routine violence. Buddy Green just shakes his head. At about that very moment, a black BMW crashes into a nearby streetlight. The driver's side is riddled with bullet holes.

With a tear in his eye Buddy Green laments, "What in the hell is wrong with young black men these days?" All of a sudden a figure comes running from directly across the street. Buddy realizes that it is Nathaniel Smith. "What happened?" asked Nathaniel. He said," Where are the police when you need them?

Someone call 9-1-1. In times past, we had to deal with the KKK, NOW BROTHERS ARE ELIMINATING BROTHERS, talk about the white man's dream?!?

Mr. Smith reaches into the car to check the driver's pulse. "Is he alive?" asks Buddy Green. "No, he appears to be dead," says Mr. Smith. The door of Prince Bern's store opens up just behind Buddy Green. Kevin Davis walks out. "Hey, that looks just like Lil' Black's car to take a closer look at the figure that slumped over that steering column. "Yes, that's Lil' Black alright. He looks dead as hell." "A bullet appears to have struck him in the head", said Mr. Smith. "My guess is that he's dead. I couldn't find a pulse. Do you know this guy?" he asks Kevin. "Sure, I do," say Kevin. Buddy says," He's one of the Big Ballers of this neighborhood." "What's a Big Baller?" asks Mr. Smith. "A drug dealer", replies Buddy Green. "Guess this serves him right", said Mr. Smith.

"You live fast, you die fast. He has done his share of killing in the community; because of guys like him the black community, as a whole is just going right down the toilet. Fathers are using or abusing drugs, mothers working two or three jobs' trying to make up the slack. And because, both parents aren't around; kids are raising themselves; with the streets as their only guide. In the process, the black family, as a whole, is an endangered species, the white man's dream. Our communities have gone from sugar to shit. We have replaced good ole' values with material things. Most of the kids now a days want to emulate 'Ballers' or hustlers' as I call them," said Buddy Green. "Lots of money, lots of flash, getting it fast and spending it even faster; that's no way to live. It'll just get you an early exit from this life, whether you go to jail or get killed. Is this what you want out of life, Kelvin?"

"You bet your ass I do," replies Kelvin, with a Swisher blunt now in hand. "Boy, sit down on this crate and let me tell you a story," said Buddy Green. "I ain't got time for any stories old man," said Kevin. "Yeah, that's right, live fast, "said Buddy Green, "don't forget the last part, and die fast." He said, "Sit your butt down boy, you've got time. How much depends on you. Lil,' Black over there didn't have time either."

"I've been sitting on this corner now for twenty odd years. I've seen 'hustlers' come and go. Out of all these years, the drug dealer is the worst hustler of the bunch. He'll sell to everyone even his family, but he don't realize, it comes full circle eventually. The drug dealer never has a solid plan either, as fast as he is making the money; he's spending it [mostly on the wrong things]. He never has plans to get out of the drug racket, because mainly, he doesn't know how. He just keeps hustling and spending and the cycle gets more and more vicious every day. That is until; he either gets busted by the cops or killed. If he was to just take some of the money, he's blowing and start a business, then he'd have something to fall back on; in case he decides to get out the game. A clothing store, car wash, or beauty shop, something to really show for all of his hustling. The white man loves this vicious cycle. In essence, it is genocide to the black community." "I don't mean to interrupt you old man," said Kelvin, "but that's the nature of the game." "Life is not a game young man, "retorted Buddy Green. He said, "Life is real. Games are bought at toy stores. If the drug game doesn't kill you, it will kill all around you, then all that is left is you, and you can't vote, can't buy a gun, and can't get a loan. See what I'm saying?"

"There is more to life than having fun, while at the same time you and your being wiped out slowly, but surly. Think about it young man, you have more choices, Lil' Black doesn't. Remember this: back in the day the KKK would lynch you, recently the cops and the judicial system were lynching you, now they can sit back and let blacks lynch each other. I've been sitting here all this time watching. I've seen a lot young man, but one thing I can tell you is with all the hustling that I've done in my day, I can honestly say that I've never sold drugs. I have never been a participant of killing my own kind, so take my advice, go to college and get a degree in something or go learn a trade, and then you'll be an asset to your neighborhood, not another casualty. Good, decent black men are very hard to find now a days."

Buddy said, "Damn, pops you certainly ran that down to me.", said Kelvin. At that moment, the sound of sirens drowned out their conversation. The police and an ambulance have finally arrived on the scene. "That's a damn shame," said Buddy Green. "It's been well over an hour since the shooting. They probably figured that it was just another nigger. If this had been one of those fancy- shamancy white neighbor hoods, they would have been on the scene long ago. Just as well thou, that brother is long gone." "Remember this picture you have in front of you young man. "That could be you slumped over that steering wheel over there."

Kevin crumbles up the blunt and walks off, head down. Thinking, Buddy Green smiles.

Education is the Best Defense

It was a bright and sunny morning in the middle of May, on the corner of 5th and Sexton; just behind Prince Bern's Party Store. There were seven kids behind the store. And they were attempting to put up a homemade basketball rim. They had a crate and were trying to bust the bottom out of it with bricks and a piece of pipe. As they were beginning to make some progress; they suddenly heard some-one shouting. "Hey, just what do you kids think you are doing?" What are you doing with my crate?"

Startled, the kids turned around quickly. They just knew it had to be the store owner. But it wasn't. It was Buddy Green, the old man who is always sitting in front of the store. "What do you mean your crate? One of the kids by the name of Lorenzo Robinson asks, "Your name isn't Borden (the name on the side of the crate) and you're not old man Bern."

"Don't sass me boy", Buddy Green annoyingly retorted. "I've been sitting on those crates for years. T has my butt print all over them." Well you don't have to worry about your butt print being on this one anymore." Lorenzo shouted back. Then he said," Cause we just knocked the bottom out of this one. Besides, old man, we only need one crate." "What are you young fellows going to do with that one crate?" asked Buddy. "We're going to attach it to that pole over there somehow and make us a basketball rim" Lorenzo replied.

"Here boys, let me help you," said Buddy Green. "I'll show you how an old pro does it." So with Buddy Green's help the crate was attached to the pole in the lot. "Now that's a hoop" Buddy Green said with a sense of glee after they'd finished putting the rim up. "Now pass me the ball. Let me show you what else the old man can do." So, Lorenzo gave Buddy Green a nice bounce pass; with which Buddy took a couple of dribbles and threw up a one-handed rainbow of a shot. The ball seemed to hang in the air forever, and then down it came. Swish! It barely touched the sides of the crate.

"Wow!" All the boys echoed at the same time. Buddy Green was still posing, his hand still in the air, and one leg still up. "That was luck," Lorenzo yelled. You can't do that again?" "Boy, you don't realize who you're talking to", shot back Buddy Green. "I was the neighborhood phenomenon growing up." "Yeah right", said Lorenzo. "Your game can't touch mine. MAN, I got the total package, mad handles, jumper, dunking, you name it."

"But you ain't said nothing about defense." said Buddy. "Let's play a little one on one, me and you." "You don't want none of this old-timer.", boasted Lorenzo.

"Sure I do," said Buddy. "First one to hit three baskets wins." "Buddy two hands a firm pass to Lorenzo's chest. He catches it, but it makes him take a slight step backwards,

Education is the Best Defense

because of the force behind it. Lorenzo starts to dribble the ball. Buddy Green gets down in a defensive posture. Lorenzo dribbles behind his back, between his legs, and crosses over a couple of times.

"Come on boy," yells Buddy. Then he said, "This ain't no dribbling clinic." Lorenzo starts toward Buddy, still dribbling the ball. He crosses him over a couple of times, and then heads toward the hoop. Slam! The other boys go berserk! "Yes", screams Lorenzo. "What I tell you, old man? You can't do nothing with me!" The other boys are nearly on the ground, whooping and hollering. "Last time, I checked that only counts as one basket", said Buddy. He said, "It's still your ball." By this time, Lorenzo is starting to feel his oats. "I' tried to warn you old man." "Just bring it", says Buddy. So, Lorenzo starts his fancy handling again. He crosses Buddy up a couple more times, and then heads for the hoop. Buddy is right with him; as Lorenzo raises the ball toward the direction of the basket. Buddy Green reaches in strips him of the ball. "Foul!" yells Lorenzo. "That's a foul!"

Buddy Green gives him the ball back without saying a word. By this time Lorenzo's friends had grown quiet. You could hear a pin drop. Lorenzo takes the ball and tries to cross Buddy up again, but Buddy reaches in and rips him of the ball. Now, Lorenzo is steamed. Buddy takes the ball out. He passes the ball to Lorenzo and yells, "check. Lorenzo tosses it back, still mad.

Buddy puts up another one-handed rainbow. Swish, yet again. "You lucky mother,****" shouts Lorenzo. "Let's see you do that again." Buddy gives him another check of the ball. JUST AS Lorenzo passes it back; Buddy makes a quick dribble and steps toward Lorenzo. Lorenzo backs up quickly. Buddy dribbles the ball back between his legs and steps back, and then lets another one-handed rainbow fly. Swish! The other boys are definitely quiet now. Lorenzo is hot! "One more basket and that's game," says Buddy. As Lorenzo was giving the ball back; after the next check he received from Buddy, he got on Buddy right away. He was determined not to let him get off a free shot.

So, Buddy started dribbling and backing into Lorenzo. Lorenzo wasn't strong enough to totally stand his ground. So, when Buddy backed him into about ten feet from the basket; he nonchalantly threw a hook shot up that went straight in.

Buddy Green pumped his fist. Lorenzo kicked the ball. His boys were speechless. "That's what I was talking about; when I said defense, young man.", Buddy Green said. He gestured for all the boys to gather around.

"You see, all of you looked at me like I had no type of B-ball skills. I used to be one of the greatest to ever come from these parts. I was just like you.

He pointed to Lorenzo. He goes on to say, "When I was growing up. I was all world in hoops. Major colleges from all over wanted me. That is until; they found out that I couldn't read. Then, no one would touch me. All my dreams… flushed right down the toilet; because I couldn't read. That's why, when you hear the grown-ups stress about grades; they're just looking out for you. The

Education is the Best Defense

world is 'dog-eat-dog'. If you can't stand on your own; (and without a good education you can't.) You will get eaten alive by these streets. So, buckle down while you're still young and make something of yourselves; that you can fall back on, if you don't make the NBA. I WISH I HAD, Then I wouldn't be sitting on this corner every day. This is no way to live, and you young man, work on your defense."

As Buddy walked away, the kids go to hoping again. Buddy went back and assumed his position in front of Bern's Party Store. He smiled as he thought of fond memories of when he was in his heydays. He always checked on those kids, too, who seemed to practice their craft every day, rain, sleet or shine. Maybe one out of the whole bunch actually heard the lesson that I was trying to teach. Maybe one won't get eaten alive by these streets. Maybe one! "I'm getting to old', Buddy thought to himself. **"WHEW, MY BACK'**!!!

Candice Blood

Candice Blood

It was a partly sunny yet overcast Fourth of July on the corner of 5th and Sexton. Buddy Green was perched on top of his usual stack of crates in front of Prince Bern's Party Store. Buddy's focus at that moment was on fond memories of his family. He was thinking about all the good times they shared. He was humming an old O' Jay's tune to himself and smiling.

All of a sudden, a car came out of nowhere. It came to a screeching halt just a few yards up the street, past Buddy. The reverse lights came on and the vehicle backed up slowly towards Buddy. It looked like a 2002 or 2003 Fleetwood Cadillac, a metallic green color, with tinted windows. The glass was dark enough for Buddy not to be able to make out; who was in it. At that point, Buddy began to sweat a little. He thought of making a break for it, but where? The car wasn't too far away from him; so if anyone was planning on doing him harm; they had the opportunity to do so. So, he stayed put. The car pulled up right in front of him. After what seemed like an eternity to Buddy; the passenger window slowly started to lower.

"What's happenin' ole' man? Came a voice from within the car. Buddy couldn't believe his eyes. "What's up fellas?" Buddy hollered back. It was Don Grace and Willie Grant, a couple of Buddy's old hangout partners from back in the day. "What'cha doing sitting' on this corner?" Don asked. "Just chilling", replied Buddy. "Nice ride. That's you Willie?"

"Yeah blood, it's me. You know I always do things in style." "Same ole' Willie", replied Buddy. "What 'you all doing in town?" "We both just got in from L.A., said Willie; we have a taste for some ribs. How 'bout you hop in and let's go get something to eat."

"Hold up, said Buddy. "Let me run inside and get a pint for ole' time's sake." "I'm buying, "shouted Don. Buddy goes and gets the pint and hops in the Caddy with his 'boys'. "This is a really nice car," said Buddy. "Bout the only thing my ex-wife didn't take from me after the divorce," said Willie. "So, how did your niece die?" asked Buddy. "Candice was killed by her ex," said Don. "Isn't that just crazy, as Hell! These young Bucks' If a woman doesn't want you anymore' you're supposed to suck it up and keep on stepping. There are more fish in the sea. They act like there's no more women left in the world. They don't even think twice now a day; about hitting or even killing women. My niece Candice had a baby by this knucklehead. I guess he just couldn't take it; when she wanted to break off the relationship. He shot her three or four times, then tried to kill himself. But, damn it, he didn't die! They have him locked up over in the county awaiting the trail; but I say forget a trail. Turn him loose and let the family get a piece of him. It'll be like giving a T-Bone to a Pit!" "I'm sorry to hear about that," said Buddy Green, as he took a swallow of the Bumpy Face;

then passed it to Don.

"I have two daughters myself. I don't know exactly, what I would do to the punk if he was to hurt one of them. Right now, I can honestly say it would be ugly; if I got my hands on 'em." 'I have a daughter that gives man her car, then calls me to get a ride to work, because she can't find him," said Willie.

Then he said, "it's not like the lazy bastard is at work on nothing'. He slings dope for a living," and no matter what I tell my daughter; she won't leave him alone. I just pray that she; one day wakes up and smell the coffee, because it's too late." "It's not like it used to be back in the day.' said Buddy. As, he is shaking his head; "A man wasn't a man back in the day; if he wasn't bringing home the bread, and the momma would make it stretch. Nobody went without! Hell, a lot of times, the neighborhood kids would get fed too. I remember many times eating at your homes, and the two of you ate at mine. Father's taught sons to be men. Mommas taught daughters to be ladies. Between, the two of them, they polished the edges, letting little girls rough, making sure little boys; knew not to hit the girls, and so on. We don't have enough people around now; that are still teaching the basics. Mommas are having to the daddy and momma; which mean she's not around to teach the kids. Mainly, because she has to go out and support the family; since daddy isn't around. He's either locked up, strung out, dicking the Friend of the Court, or dead.

It's a very ugly situation, and not many people are

paying close attention. This situation is mainly; in the black neighborhoods. There are fewer and fewer black families left. It is truly genocide from within, and don't think for one moment that this wasn't all part of 'the big plan' and a bunch of these suckass out here are fallin' right in the trap."

The three of them rode around for hours, reminiscing about their younger days. "I have an idea," said Buddy. Then he said, "Let's have our own barbeque tomorrow. We can have one celebrating your niece Candice moving' to heaven above. Black folks don't do that much anymore, but you're supposed to celebrate. It's still big down in Louisiana." "I think that would be a good idea", said Don. "It will get everyone out of their sadness somewhat."

"Just drop me off at my crib", said Buddy. "I still live in the old house that I grew up in, my mother passed it on to me when she died." When the Caddy pulled up to Buddy's house the entire neighborhood was gawking. When Buddy got out, some of them whooped and hollered.

"Hey Buddy, sweet ride." one of them said. "Ain't nothing but a thang." said Buddy Green. As he turned to go in the house, Buddy said to his boys', "Pick me up about 8a.m. 'I'LL FIX MY SPECIALTY.' Hey Don, I want to go to the funeral, too. When is it?" "It's being held this Friday. We'd be honored to have you there. See you in the morning man." "Yeah, see you in the morning blood." Willie said.

Buddy Green went into the house. He went to work right away; preparing for the barbeque and the funeral.

[The End]
Rodney R. Rhodes

Email: Blackifiedllc@yahoo.com
Website: RodneyRRhodes.com

Printed in the USA
CPSIA information can be obtained
at www.ICGtesting.com
CBHW050409070824
12782CB00044B/793